FOCUSED RIDING

Focused Riding

Robert J. Schinke
Beverley Schinke

COMPASS EQUESTRIAN
LONDON

Drawings by Sally Bell
Edited by Martin Diggle
Designed by Hugh Johnson

Published in Great Britain in 1997 by
Compass Equestrian Limited
Eardley House
4 Uxbridge Street
Farm Place
London W8 7SY

ISBN 1 900667 56 8

A catalogue record for this book is available
from the British Library

Printed in Great Britain by
Biddles Ltd
Guilford

Contents

LIST OF FIGURES

DEDICATION

To Wolfgang Schinke, who invited us to share his dream
and dedicated his life to making it a reality.
With love, Robert and Beverley.

ACKNOWLEDGEMENTS

We would like to acknowledge all the riding students and coaches who
have touched our lives, and whose lives we have touched.
In addition, we would also like to thank several people for their
friendship and professional support over the years. Those whose help
was invaluable are, in alphabetical order : Denny Emerson, Kate
Green, Jim Henry, Bertie Hill, Jack LeGoff, Ian Millar, Sue Ockendon,
Mark Phillips, Ole Sorensen and Cara Whitham.
We would also like to thank our academic mentors:
Dr Jean-Marie Beniskos, Dr Ann Hall, Dr Terry Orlick,
Dr Wendy Rodgers and Dr John Salmela.
Finally, we wish to acknowledge the four generations of our family
who share our love of horses and riding.

PREFACE

Everyone has their own goals that they hope to attain through riding. Some people want to learn the fundamentals so that they can eventually take leisurely rides in the countryside. Others sign on for consecutive series of riding lessons in order to master the arts of dressage and jumping, and there are those who aspire mainly to compete. Regardless of a rider's objectives, planning is required. Things don't just happen – whether we are conscious of it or not, events unfold. Sport psychology provides several of the tools necessary to ensure that our objectives are met. Here is a sample of some of the questions that have been raised in the past:

- What am I trying to achieve in this ride?
- How do I further improve my confidence?
- How can I refine my concentration techniques during training and competitions?
- Are there concrete ways of assessing my improvement?
- How can I ride consistently to my potential?

This book offers training techniques which will help you to deal with these and other eventualities. When we were younger, we unknowingly practised some of these techniques. For instance, as school children, some of us were chastised for day-dreaming. Others had visions of ourselves in the future achieving 'impossible things'. Others yet were seen as 'over-confident'. In our childhood, we had the natural capabilities to imagine, and to believe in ourselves. However, some of this behaviour was seen as inappropriate at the time and as we grew older, most of us misplaced these abilities. Now, however, you may wish to retrieve these skills and use them to enhance your performance. Those gifts which came to us so naturally as children are today referred to as 'sport psychology methodologies'. When we learn the procedures and call upon these gifts, they cease to be the almost random behaviour of childhood, and become tools which enable us to achieve mastery of ourselves and our sport.

Each technique learned becomes a tool of our trade and, as we acquire further skills, they become part of our sport psychology 'tool box'. A tool box is a handy thing, filled with implements that make life simpler. As we become familiar with its contents, we become handier with their usage. Our first efforts may be clumsy — sometimes, we may pick up the wrong tool but, over time and with practice, we learn the benefits of each. So it is with sport psychology methods. Some of them sound too easy to be true; others appear too difficult to grasp. As with other skills, in the beginning most tools feel uncomfortable and awkward. Why, if we did these things so naturally as children, do they feel so uncomfortable now? The answer is simple: because we are calling on unpractised skills and employing them in unfamiliar settings. With time and practice, the skills that you thought you had lost will become valuable tools in your equestrian pursuits.

At this point, we would like to emphasise the importance of practice. It has been our experience that many people call on sport psychology skills intermittently. However, to be at their most useful, the strategies must be developed and refined on a daily basis over a period of time. In this book, each chapter explains a specific mental skill in detail, and also provides a number of Tasks, which pose questions and suggest actions relevant to the acquisition of these skills. The purpose of these Tasks is to prompt you to think deeply about the ideas discussed, and to provide a practical framework by which they can be incorporated into your repertoire of riding skills. We would suggest, therefore, that you give serious consideration to the issues raised, record your responses in a notebook, and refer to them as you continue the pursuit of your riding objectives.

At the end of each chapter, we have also added a list of suggested Further Reading, detailing other material complementary to the ideas discussed in this book.

It is our fervent hope that this book proves helpful to you in your pursuit of riding enjoyment and excellence. We are delighted to have the opportunity to share some ideas with you, and welcome you on what we promise will be an exciting journey.

Trouble-shooting

The specific mental skills explained in this book are dealt with sequentially, each of them building on the subject matter that precedes it. Therefore, when you settle down to read the book, we recommend that you do so chapter-by-chapter. We are aware, however, that many people first embrace sport psychology because they wish to deal with one particular problem. Here is a list of problems that we are often consulted about, each with a chapter reference to show that this book can help you to solve it, if it happens to be a problem that affects you.

Problem	Chapter(s)
How can I make unfamilar challenges familiar?	Chapter 2
I can't get confident enough to do what I want to do.	Chapters 2 and 6
I love to jump, but I'm afraid of new fences.	Chapters 6 and 9
I get competition jitters.	Chapter 5 – Relaxation
Are there any quick methods that I can use to relax?	Chapter 5
How can I relax my horse?	Chapters 5 and 8
I can't stop yawning at competitions.	Chapter 5 – Activation
I am easily distracted.	Chapter 4
I'm stressed out. Help!	Chapters 4, 5 and 8
I feel so rushed. How do I manage my time better?	Chapter 8
How do I get better organized at competitions?	Chapter 7
How can I make people believe in me?	Chapter 8
How do I learn a new skill?	Chapter 6
How can I develop an optimal support team?	Chapter 7
How will I know when I have reached my full potential?	Chapters 3 and 9

CHAPTER 1
GETTING STARTED

*A journey of a thousand miles
begins with a footstep.*
Tao Te Ching No.64

When reflecting back to rides we have had in the past, we may note that some have felt light and responsive, while others were heavy and mechanical. Interestingly, both these sensations probably occurred for the same horse-rider combination over the course of their partnership. Often, our objective is to reproduce best-ever rides, and avoid those which are less successful. As we become more consistent in our partnerships, we realize that positive rides are easily recaptured, and negative ones more readily avoided. However, to achieve these aims we require an organized plan, in which personal emotions and mental strategies play a large part. In essence, becoming a complete performer requires a balance between technical knowledge and kinesthetic application for horse and rider to become one. (The kinesthetic sense governs our awareness of our own body, and that of our horse, and is often referred to as 'feel'. It is essentially a physical sense, the product of signals sent by tiny nerve bodies in response to movements of our joints and muscle endings. This sense, as a whole, enables us to remain subconsciously aware of where our body parts are in relation to each other. Since our emotions and mental images can have physical effects upon our bodies, they can consequently affect our kinesthetic sense, and that of our horse.)

Sport psychology enables us to combine our mental processes and emotions with our physical skills, so that we can apply our whole selves positively, to optimum effect. Together, the mind, body, and soul help us reach our potential in our chosen sport. Put simply, sport psychology is a set of tools which, integrated into our daily lives, will help us perform to our potential consistently

What, then, are the component elements of sport psychology? To be

successful, we need to develop:
- A mental game plan that includes clear and realistic goals.
- A positive-performance image.
- focused attention.
- An optimal balance between activation and relaxation.
- A balanced lifestyle.

and, finally, the ability to combine all of these into a system that works.

Riders often ask whether sport psychology skills would enhance their performance. The answer is that few sports require so much mental strategy as riding. For one thing, it is an interactive sport between two unique entities – the rider and the horse. Our communications with horses are carried out through body signals and spoken words. When we ask our horses to perform, we do so carefully, in order to communicate our needs without compromising the spirit of our partners. The winning combination, be it in leisure or competition, performs together in the pleasant harmony that we all like to consider a partnership.

The winning combination, be it in leisure or competition, performs together in the pleasant harmony that we all like to consider a partnership.

When horse and rider perform at their best, it is the result of a shared vision (that is, the horse enjoys doing what is required of him), the correct energy level, and an organized mental procedure. Indeed, these factors are the hallmarks of a successful horse – rider combination.

At a recreational level, the strategy might be directed towards riding proficiently for the purposes of enjoyment and relaxation. For competitors, the strategy remains directed at improving performance, with the additional goal of positive competition results. Interestingly, both groups of people require similar strategies in order to improve their rides – and those who are most content with their equestrian pursuits (whatever these may be) seem to have an understanding of how their riding has progressed to the present, a clear view of where to go next, and an understanding of how to get there. Furthermore, the most successful riders also know how to bring out the best in themselves and their mounts at a given time in order to achieve their objectives. This ability is developed from personal awareness and past experience.

DEFINING MENTAL STRATEGIES

Before discussing the various mental training strategies in detail during the following chapters, let us provide you with a definition and basic understanding of each.

GOAL-SETTING

Goal-setting is the reference point which directs all other mental training skills. Goals are simply the objectives we want to achieve in every aspect of our lives, be it riding, business, school, or personal matters. When we ride, the objective might be to reward ourselves after a day of office work, to improve physical fitness, to learn a specific riding skill, or to win an Olympic medal. Each of these are specific goals that we choose as individuals. Long-term goals help us to establish the direction in which our riding can develop. Short-term goals are methods of monitoring our progress towards the long-term objectives. For instance, those who are Young Riders in eventing may well identify becoming a successful senior National Team member as a four-year objective. To achieve this long-term goal, they could choose to enter Young Riders Selection Trials and see how they fare against other aspiring eventers. This will provide a clearer understanding of what needs to be improved. The identification of interim goals directs them closer to their long-term objectives.

Once result-based goals are selected, the next step is to identify the skills and techniques that need to be developed and refined in order to attain these goals. Such objectives are called process-directed goals. It is through the combination of result-based and process-directed goals that we reach our dreams.

IMAGERY

Once goals have been identified, the next logical step is to begin treating each goal through your mind's eye and body as if it were real. This process is known as imagery, or mental rehearsal, and it is probably the most commonly taught sport psychology exercise. At the highest level, imagery involves four of our senses (seeing, touching, hearing and smelling) to create a vivid and exact replica of the actual equestrian experience. The objectives of imagery vary from providing a positive direction toward short- and long-term performance objectives to developing and maintaining personal confidence for a forthcoming task. For instance, a novice rider who is venturing outside the arena for the first time might want to visualize the ride before attempting it. By doing so, the rider will affirm a capability to ride outdoors while also becoming mentally familiar with the experience. Thus, the actual experience becomes familiar before it is ever undertaken.

RELAXATION SKILLS

These are tools you can employ to shift mentally from an angry, nervous or serious mode into a clearer and more comforting way of thinking. Have you ever heard of breathing exercises or progressive muscle relaxation? These are two of many relaxation skills you could employ when trying to settle your nerves and focus your mind. Other relaxation skills include utilizing activities that restore your positive energy such as listening to soft music, meditating, taking some quiet time for yourself when needed, or engaging in activities with family and friends who tend to rejuvenate and reinforce a positive state of mind.

STATES OF ACTIVATION

There are varying levels of energy at which we perform. Some of us are always calm and easygoing: others are highly strung, and sometimes over-energized. Through employing the correct sport psychology techniques, we ascertain which level of activation works best for us and our horses for specific disciplines and riding objectives. For instance, nervous recreational riders wanting a relaxing ride in the countryside will need to lower their energy level with relaxation exercises before beginning their ride. When the correct energy level is achieved by a rider, the riding experience becomes smooth, settled, and enjoyable. It is important to understand that we all have the ability to increase and decrease our energy levels for each sporting context and discipline.

FOCUSING SKILLS

The ability to focus our minds is central in the development of a mental skills package. Focusing skills are exercises, or 'tasks', that get those who use them centred on what they are preparing to do before each ride. One example of focusing entails selecting appropriate cue words to bring one's attention from a diffused, 'floodlight' perspective to a more concentrated 'spotlight' orientation. For some riders, the words 'centre' or 'here' are sufficient to refocus them onto the task at hand. Other methods of improving concentration include deliberately riding with distractions, and establishing strategies to cope with them. The precise focusing skills used will vary depending on the individual, the equestrian discipline, the horse and the sporting context.

PRE-COMPETITION STRATEGIES

These are formalized plans of how to evaluate situations, prepare for them and facilitate peak performances. For the competitive rider, some of the ingredients of pre-competition strategies will include simulating each respective discipline one dressage movement or jump at a time and then combining all the components into a complete simulated dressage or jumping test. Another technique of pre-competition preparation is identifying short-term goals with which to direct expectation levels for a forthcoming performance. Other components that are central to pre-competition packages include developing a packing list, preparing a suitable show ground regime for yourself and your horse, and agreeing on a communication process with your trainer, support staff and team members that enhances, rather than hinders, performance.

EXHIBITION PACKAGE

On arrival at a competition site, an exhibition package can be employed. The components of this will vary from one horse–rider combination to another, but may include how and when you off-load your horse from the trailer, how you familiarize yourself with unfamiliar grounds, and how you greet fellow competitors and officials. Beyond this, the exhibition package also includes personal warm-up procedures for general workouts, immediate pre-competition warm-ups, and the mental skills that can be employed before and during each competition performance.

PROCEDURE SETTING AND JOURNAL KEEPING

Procedure setting is a systematic method of establishing a sense of control over competitive situations. When reading the autobiographies of international riders, and performers in other sports, it becomes evident that many of them dress in a particular sequence, nap for a specific time prior to commencing warm-ups, eat certain foods, listen to special music, and visualize their performances in a specific way and at specific times during competitions. How do these activities tie in with journal keeping? Journals are a means of identifying those aspects and procedures

When reading the autobiographies of international riders it becomes evident that many of them dress in a particular sequence.

of training and competing that work well for your horse–rider partnership, and those that have been detrimental in the past. Inevitably, those components of your routines that do work become part of your competition procedures, whereas those that fail are revised, or avoided during future rides.

PEAKS, VALLEYS AND PLATEAUX

Even though each of the aforementioned strategies plays an important role in performance enhancement, it is inevitable that every rider will experience peaks, valleys and plateaux in their riding careers. Indeed, these are inevitable parts of the learning process. Whilst a new skill is being acquired, it may initially be accompanied by a decrease in performance quality (a valley). Later, while the skill is in the process of becoming automated, many of us reach a plateau – an opportunity to integrate new lessons. Once we have become proficient at the desired skill, we begin to apply it in our own unique way. It is during this stage that we may reach a peak in our riding experiences.

BALANCED PERSPECTIVE

This is the ability to develop an approach to sport and life that combines hobbies with professional and personal responsibilities. The mature weekend rider will probably allocate time for recreational pursuits, family, and friends. With the top-level or professional competitor, more time is spent on riding, so many spend their leisure time in activities unrelated to horses. When riders attempt to balance their lives in such a way, they often find that their riding and occupational time become more productive. On the other hand, some people focus on one specific aspect of their lives at the expense of other priorities. In Chapter 8 issues such as prioritizing and stress and time management will be discussed. The strategy for each will emphasize the importance of a holistic approach to sport and life, in order to ensure continued success in your equestrian endeavours.

You will no doubt have recognized that many of the aforementioned strategies are familiar to you. Throughout the rest of this book, the components mentioned will be explained in detail and discussed in equestrian contexts, so that they can be applied across all equestrian disciplines. As you attempt each skill and its prescribed exercises, do not be discouraged if results do not materialize instantly – remember that mental skills are cultivated and developed like physical skills, and thus require time and perseverance. As you practise your mental skills regularly, you will find that they and your physical skills will improve concurrently. Furthermore, with each step you take in improving your mental skills, you will gain a better understanding of why, when and how to call on these mental tools.

Task 1. For now, take the opportunity to re-examine some of the mental skills outlined above. Consider how many of the components you have used up to the present, and how many others might enhance your performance in both training and competition. When you are ready, turn the page and we can begin our journey together.

FURTHER READING

Cox, R., Qui, Y., and Liu, Z. ' Overview of sport psychology' in R. N. Singer, M. Murphey and L. K. Tennant (eds.), *Handbook of research on sport psychology*, (New York, Macmillan 1993), pp. 3-31.

Schinke, R. J 'A general understanding of sport psychology concepts for elite equestrians', *Australian Horse & Rider*, vol.5, (1995), pp. 24-6.

CHAPTER 2
IMAGINE RIDING

If you have a dream alive in your mind,
bring it to the world, give it life....
For even if only a few people
benefit from our offering, the world
is then a better place to live.
Susan Staszewski

Every person has imagination; the ability to image. In a recent sport psychology symposium, we asked seventy-five Young Riders whether they had ever attempted imagery. From their responses, only six people in the audience believed that they had done so. The remaining sixty-nine people in the room were convinced that they had never used imagery in their lives. In order to illustrate that we all call on some form of mental rehearsal, the riders were enlisted as reluctant participants in a little experiment. They were asked to close their eyes and listen as we described various tastes, feelings and situations. For example, as one exercise, we asked our group to imagine themselves biting into a sour lemon. Before long, everyone in the group was puckering their lips in response to the bitter taste described. During a second scenario, we explored the kinesthetic senses by having the riders imagine that they were diving into a lake where cold water engulfed their bodies. In response to this description everyone, without exception, shivered.

Throughout the discussion, we called on experiences that we knew would be common to the people attending our workshop. To ensure that the imagery remained successful from one scenario to the next, we made sure to emphasize at least one of the five senses, and preferably more, as part of each description. Needless to say, before long, we had seventy-five keen Young Riders, who were excited and sold on their own ability to use the imaging technique

For many riders, both recreational and competitive, imagery is associated solely with the ability to visualize themselves performing either

We explored the kinesthetic senses by having the riders imagine that they were diving into a lake where cold water engulfed them.

as if they were on the horse, or else watching the performance on a video screen. Although this form of imagery is beneficial, the best quality imagery extends beyond visual cues into a multi-sensual experience, where touch and sound also become part of the process. An example of complete imagery for a dressage rider should include a combination of several senses employed concurrently. Visually, the rider should see the horse's neck, the dressage arena and its markers, their own forearms, hands, and the reins. At the same time, the rider should hear the horse's rhythm, be it at walk, trot, canter, piaffe or tempi changes. There is also the rider's own kinesthetic body awareness. For instance, how much pressure is exerted from both leg and hand, whether the seat is deep in the saddle, whether the rider's lower back is supple or stiff, and whether the horse is light and responsive to the aids.

There are also other relevant kinesthetic cues such as personal breathing pattern; whether this is shallow or deep, regular or intermittent, forced or easy. Finally, based on the imagery cues, the rider's confidence is either enhanced or diminished.

A GUIDED INTRODUCTION TO IMAGERY

Now that we have explained some of the intricacies of practising imagery, it is time to introduce you to the experience. Before attempting the forthcoming exercise, allow yourself the time and space to complete it properly. If you don't have the full fifteen or twenty minutes at this moment, wait until a quiet time presents itself.

Task 2. Before going any further in this chapter, we are going to take you through a guided imagery exercise. In order for it to be effective, please follow these suggestions:

- Loosen all clothing until it is comfortable.
- Find a comfortable place to sit down – preferably a surface that is only as hard as your saddle.
- Close your eyes (after you have first read the following instructions!).
- Establish a regular breathing pattern by inhaling through your nose and exhaling through your mouth. This will help you relax your diaphragm and take in deep breaths of air. Take five deep breaths, hold each one for five seconds, and then exhale.
- Whenever you are ready, have a friend or family member read the following exercise to you in a soft and relaxed tone. Also, you might want to add some soft New Age music (preferably with nature sounds) to enhance the ensuing scenario.
- Release your mind to the exercise, and become one with the experience.

Guided imagery for relaxation and recreation

There is nowhere you need to go and nothing you need to do. This is your time to relax your body and your mind. Breathe in through your nose. Hold. Breathe out (repeat five times). Imagine yourself in a warm, sunny place. It is not too hot, just nice and warm. You feel the sun soaking into your skin and warming your body. You are completely at peace with yourself and everything around you. There is a gentle breeze, and you can smell the beginning of summer. The trees are a deep green and the leaves are whispering as the breeze blows gently through the branches. There is a beautiful barn, and in it the most wonderfully gentle and responsive horse you can imagine. Notice how Nature is inviting you to take the horse for a relaxing hack in the nearby fields and distant woods. It's just the perfect day for a ride.

Someone has thoughtfully tacked up the horse for you. Notice how the horse's coat shines in the sun and how the horse moves so gracefully as he is led towards you. You can hear the sound of the horse's hooves as he happily approaches you. You take the reins in one hand, put your other hand on the saddle, your foot in the stirrup and swing gently into the saddle. As you settle yourself in the saddle, notice the scent of the leather and the horse, and how these combine with the scent of grass, flowers, and trees. Feel the sun on your back as you begin to walk towards that beautiful track. As you draw nearer, quietly ask your horse to trot. As you move through the forest in a soft rising trot, feel the two-beat rhythm of the movement. The horse's ears are pricked for-ward and his hindquarters are swinging gently. You seem to be breath-ing in unison with your horse. After a little while, gently give the aid to canter and feel the soft, rolling motion of the gait. The horse has picked up the canter easily and is moving steadily onward with you. You can hear and feel the change to the three-beat rhythm. You can feel the breeze on your skin, and you notice the forest in all its glory. Breathe in the scent of the forest and allow it to relax you with its per-fect fragrance. You are one with your horse and with Nature. Enjoy your ride... (reader pauses for about 10 seconds).

This is what you love about riding – the calm, quiet partnership. Now you see a meadow up ahead with a pond, and you slow to a trot and then a walk. Your horse makes his way quietly to the pond and leans down for a cool sip of water. Notice the sound of the water splashing slightly as the horse drinks. You stretch too – you feel marvellously at peace and relaxed.

After a while you notice that the sun is beginning to set, and the sky is beginning to take on a pinkish orange hue. You pick up your reins slowly and start to walk. Then, as you head back to the barn, you sig-nal the horse into a nice, easy trot. You are enjoying the scenery as you return and you can hear the twigs and leaves crunching underfoot... The barn, too soon, comes into sight. You slow the horse to a walk and upon entering the yard, you halt and dismount. As you put up your stir-rups and loosen the girth, the horse turns gently to nuzzle you, as if to thank you.

Next, you remove the tack and brush the horse before returning him to his stable. You have one more look around the barn as you prepare to leave and you take a deep breath, enjoying the horsy scent. The horse whinnies softly – 'goodbye'. It has been a wonderfully relaxing ride; the end to a perfect day...
(reader allow music to continue for an additional 30–60 seconds).

This is your special retreat, one to which you can return whenever you wish. You need only close your eyes and relax, take five deep breaths, and guide yourself back to this scenario, at will. Whenever you are ready, at your leisure, open your eyes gradually. Also, take your time getting up, so that the end of the exercise is as gradual and relaxing as the exercise itself. If you get up too quickly, you may feel dizzy.

This relaxation exercise can be used to release tension when you cannot go to the stable, or during any time of stress or pressure. The horse, barn, forest, meadow, and pond are left to your imagination. Inevitably, you will land up tailoring the image to fit your idea of perfection. The most important thing is that the exercise must be a relaxing one.

New and nervous riders, as well as more experienced competitors, can benefit from this relaxing journey of the mind and body. It will allow you to establish or recapture the feeling of a relaxed ride which will, in turn, help you remind your body and mind how to relax whilst riding. Trainers may also want to practise this exercise with new or highly strung riders, or riders dealing with difficult horses, prior to a lesson. Thus they may prescribe this exercise as part of a rider's pre-lesson preparation.

Task 3. Recalling the guided imagery described above, here are some criteria by which you can identify your imagery skills and evaluate their quality. When looking over each question, take your time before responding. You may find that you have additional criteria for each sense employed during the imagery process. If so, add these to the list, because they too will strengthen the quality of your skills. You may also find that your experiences take only a few criteria into account. If so, the remaining criteria provide you with an indication of how to improve your skills.
The visual aspects to consider include:

1. Do you visualize in black and white, grey, or colour?

2. How bright and vivid are the objects in your imagery?

3. Are the tones and colours of the images correct?

4. Is your image a still frame or moving picture?

5. If the image is a moving picture, is it moving at a true speed, too slow, or too fast?

6. Is your image centred, or is it off to one side?

7. Is the image you envisage close up or away in the distance?

8. How many dimensions does the image have? Is it flat, or does it also have depth?

9. Is the image in the third or first person (are you seeing the image as if watching a video, or from a rider's eye point of view)?

Auditory cues can also improve the quality and completeness of the imagery. For instance:

10. What sounds (if any) do you hear to complement the images you see?

11. Are the sounds that you hear loud and clear, or muffled?

12. Are the sounds regular or intermittent (for example, the rhythm of the horse's stride)?

The kinesthetic elements of body awareness are perhaps the most crucial components of the imagery process. Consider the following:

13. How do your muscles feel during the imagery? Do you feel them at all? If so, which ones? Are they the appropriate muscles?

14. Can you feel your legs, hands, seat and back connecting with the horse as they should? If so, explain the feeling; if not, identify why they are not.

15. Are you and your horse in balance during the imagery, or is either one of you leaning to one side?

16. At what speed are your muscles and your horse's muscles moving during your imagery – in slow motion, normally, or too fast?

17. How much energy and activity are associated with your own and your horse's performance?

Finally, mental components are also included in the imagery process. Their influence may give rise to points such as:

18. Are you and your horse completing your tasks successfully?

19. Do you feel confident of your own and your horse's physical skills during the imagery process?

Note that the auditory and kinesthetic elements of the imagery will vary in their importance for each rider. This is because some of us cue into visual images, others into 'feel', and others yet into sounds. In the context of riding, it is the kinesthetic, visual, and mental components that should be emphasized. Remember, however, that the ultimate objective is to include as many of the above-mentioned cues as possible in your imagery.

HOW TO DEVELOP YOUR IMAGERY SKILLS

As stated, the best way to develop and improve your imaging ability is to add as many different cues as possible to the mental rehearsal process. More often than not, the inclusion of these components occurs gradually, just like the development of most other skills. Many people begin by viewing themselves performing successfully in the third person (similar to watching oneself on a video screen). The picture itself is usually unclear, possibly in black and white, or grey, and is most often viewed as from a distance. As a person's visualizing ability improves, the picture itself becomes closer and takes on clarity and colour, thus improving its quality. Through continued practice, many experienced riders eventually 'step into' their images, and view their performance as if they were seeing it unfolding through their own eyes. With first-person imagery there come the familiar sounds and sensations experienced in an actual ride. As a result, the mental rehearsal process becomes more complete and lifelike: the rider experiences a personal involvement in the imagery rather than the initial, detached video-like perspective.

Thus, patience pays dividends when you are developing and refining your imagery skills.

SOME POSSIBLE APPLICATIONS FOR IMAGERY IN RIDING

Imagery contributes to excellent performance in many ways. In the first place, it can be employed to boost confidence before attempting a difficult movement. In essence, if you can see yourself performing the movement successfully, then a positive performance is more likely to follow than might otherwise be the case. You can also use mental rehearsal before a competition to memorize the intricacies of a performance plan, whether it be for a flat race, a point-to-point, a hunter trial, a show jumping round, a dressage test or a pleasure ride. The added familiarity with the course or route, as well as your tactics for completing it successfully, will be conducive to an improved performance.

These two applications of imagery reveal only some of its strengths. To provide you with a more comprehensive idea of its usefulness, let us consider some specific contexts in which imagery can be practised.

PRODUCING POSITIVE MENTAL IMAGES

Imagery provides the rider with a positive mental picture in times of uncertainty – whether these be during training or competition. To achieve this effect, a concerted effort must be made to picture the successful employment of the necessary skills. Often, first attempts at imagery produce negative pictures – whether of taking a show jump, riding dressage figures, or galloping over solid obstacles. Do not be discouraged, just practise the exercise until a picture of a successful performance is produced in your mind. Far too often, people produce images that are negative, such as reaching the wrong take-off point for a show jump or cross-country obstacle. When they do this, we urge them to make the correction and produce fresh images of themselves, assuming a more positive and confident approach to their riding challenges. After all, regardless of your level and objectives, a positive frame of mind is the starting point for eventual success. This being the case, it is worthwhile – indeed essential – to practise your imagery skills in order to perfect them. Therefore, commit yourself to imagery on a regular basis – twice a week minimum.

Task 4. Take five minutes, close your eyes, sit in a riding position and

see if you can form an image of yourself on your horse. In your imagery, attempt a recently acquired skill – whether it be a turn on the forehand, a new jumping exercise, or a postural correction. Start the process by taking a few deep breaths, and bring yourself gradually into the training scenario you have selected. If the imagined execution of the movement is flawed, correct yourself and repeat the exercise until it is flawless. During this exercise, remember that you have the ability to revise your images until they are to your liking.

Having completed your imagery think about the outcome. Were you able to complete the desired exercise successfully without being guided by a script?

Some people find positive mental pictures difficult to imagine. Frequently, this inability is explained by a non-availability of previous memories in their memory library. If you are in this position, mental rehearsal could usefully be coupled with video footage of previous rides. If none is available, seek out footage of other riders from the level and discipline you ride at, who are displaying the sought-after skill. If, for example, you have a certain lack of confidence in your cross-country jumping abilities, it can be very helpful to choose an aggressive, yet technically correct rider upon whom to model yourself. Just watching such a performer can reinforce your image of how positive you need to be in order to ride a successful cross-country round.

The procedure for using video footage to develop or restore confidence is quite simple. Appropriately selected footage will provide you with a positive example of how to complete the task successfully. After viewing sections of the tape, pause the video cassette and close your eyes. Imagine yourself stepping into the picture, and assume the sought-after style that you observed on tape. Work at the imagery until you see yourself producing an equally successful result. At the same time, the positive footage will serve as a reminder of how the particular discipline and its intricacies look, sound, and feel. These cues may assist in placing you back in touch with positive competition experiences.

REPLICATING PHYSICAL SENSATIONS

Imagery can be used to replicate the physical sensations usually experienced when riding in the visualized discipline. Interestingly, when athletes were observed using imagery in an experimental laboratory, it was found that their muscles and nerve fibres could not differentiate between imagery and actual physical workouts. Therefore, both forms of 'exercise' led to physical fatigue. As sport consultants, we have seen many athletes using imagery as part of their warm-up procedures. Some have done so to bring themselves to the correct energy level, and remind themselves of what was to come. Others, however, fatigued themselves through excessive use of the technique. In such cases, the

Some riders have fatigued themselves through excessive use of imagery.

performers would practise for more than an hour before attempting the actual skill or event. This entailed continuing to practise long after achieving the correct image, usually because they felt insecure in their abilities. However, doing so was unnecessary and, in many cases, proved detrimental to their performances. Therefore, while we recommend training through a combination of both mental and physical exertion, we would stress the importance of not over-training either one.

As may be evident from the above, imagery can also be used to supplement physical practice when you are unable to ride. If you ride re-creationally, and are unable to practise your skills daily, mental rehearsal exercises will attune your senses to the sport on those days when riding is not possible. For the competitive rider, similar exercises can be employed when circumstances interrupt daily training. However, it should be understood that imagery alone is not enough to improve your performance to an optimal level. All research into the contributions of physical and mental rehearsal to skilled performance has confirmed the same findings: that mental and physical rehearsal are both conducive to improved performance, but the best results always occur when both are practised regularly in tandem.

RELAXATION

The final use of imagery we should consider is to facilitate a sense of relaxation before mounting. In both recreational and competitive settings, riders often become over-activated by the potential challenges that lie ahead. For different riders these challenges might include performing a formidable show jumping test, setting out on a challenging cross-country course, trying a new dressage test in competition, or riding in an open field for the first time. In preparing for such challenges, many of the best performers have developed relaxing images to call upon before undertaking their tasks. When working with Olympic performers, we encourage them to develop a mental retreat that they can utilize in times of pressure. Doing so tends to provide a calming state prior to undertaking a major challenge or entering a stressful situation. This procedure is discussed in detail during Chapter 5.

As you will appreciate by now, imagery can play an integral role in the development of performance, whatever a rider's skill level and favoured discipline. To reiterate, if imagery is practised consistently it will provide your body and mind with a sense of familiarity with specific riding contexts, and will also enhance your confidence through the provision of a positive mental picture. These factors will inevitably help you to reach the goal of achieving peak performances consistently, whether in recreational riding, training or competition.

While the images in your mind will act as important signposts towards future goals and performances, imagery is only the starting point in the pursuit of excellence. In order to take the next step in our progression as riders, we need to establish realistic goals which lead us toward our dreams. The next chapter will explain how to take this second, very important step. For the moment, here are some reminders on the use of imagery.

REMINDERS ON IMAGERY

- Third-person (video screen) imagery is of great benefit when you want to re-establish confidence.
- When you are using first-person imagery, adopt a sitting /riding position for best results.
- When practising first-person imagery, call on as many senses as possible – the more the better.
- Relaxation imagery and mental retreat images are favoured as preparatory strategies for over-activated riders of all levels and disciplines
- Sometimes, a high performance state is required, but is difficult to envisage. In such circumstances stimulating imagery – such as watching video footage of previous performances – will be beneficial.
- When practising any form of imagery, commit yourself to two sessions per week.

FURTHER READING

Hendricks, G., and Wills, R. *The centering book*, (Englewood Cliffs, New Jersey, Prentice Hall 1975).

Lynch, J. ' Visualization', *Thinking body, dancing mind : Taosports for extraordinary performance in business, sport and life*, (New York, Bantam 1992), pp.16-23.

Schinke, R. J. ' Mental preparation for three-day event competitions', *International Eventing*, vol.12, (1995), pp. 30-1.

Schinke, R. J. ' The uses and implementation of imagery ', *Australian Horse & Rider*, vol. 6, (1995), pp. 30-2.

Suinn, R. ' Imagery', in R. N. Singer, M. Murphey, and L. K. Tennant (eds.), *Handbook of research on sport psychology*, (New York, Macmillan 1993), pp. 492-510.

CHAPTER 3
DIRECTION THROUGH GOAL-SETTING

The great thing in this world
is not so much where we are,
but in what direction we are moving.
Oliver Wendell Holmes

Wolfgang Schinke holds the view that 'every reality begins with a dream'. Every successful person whom we have encountered seems to confirm his theory. High achievers, whether they be in sport, business, or personal life, seem to have begun their journey with a long-term vision of where they wanted to be. As children, they began formulating goals at the subconscious level, perhaps in the form of day-dreams. In their youth, they learned the importance of developing their ability to concentrate, yet few were encouraged to dream. Nevertheless, most were incessant dreamers as children, and allowed their minds to wander to strange and wonderful places – they dared to dream.

As a matter of curiosity, were you ever chastized for day-dreaming? Moreover, are you still following the exciting dreams that you once set for yourself? Do these questions provoke some interesting thoughts on your part? Finally, has your life taken a direction inspired by dreams that you envisaged as a child, or by coincidence? Whatever your answers to these questions, the purpose of this chapter is to provide you with a strong conceptual understanding of goal-setting and to describe some exercises that will help you clarify, take control of, and implement your future goals.

Even as children, Melanie Smith and Bruce Davidson, Olympic gold medallists in show jumping and eventing, both aspired to become members of their national teams. Later, during their teenage years, they continued seeing themselves as future international performers. At first, their images were unfounded dreams. However, both began to take deliberate steps torwards realizing their visions. Once they achieved their goals of becoming members of their respective national equestrian teams, both established new long-term goals: to develop into leading international performers. Therein lies the difference between the consummate dreamer and the person who moves foward and meets long-term objectives. For the two riders cited, each progressive step was directed by long-term visions, and monitored with short-term stepping stones. Therefore, it can be said that goals begin as distant dreams, before being recognized as distinct possibilities, and then pursued.

PERSPECTIVES IN GOAL-SETTING

Goal-setting is closely related to the development of skills. Whether we are high-level competitors, local-level competitors, or pleasure riders, we all need to set goals to carry us forward in our pursuits. Often, we see riders who forget to reset goals and, as a result, stop their own progress. As sport psychologists, we have spent much of our time helping performers establish a meaning, and thus a direction, for their sport interests. Initial meetings often begin with people explaining that they are frustrated whilst playing their sport and no longer gaining enjoyment from it. After some discussion, it becomes apparent that they have forgotten to reset new goals once old ones have been accomplished. We explain that there is no greater reward than meeting old objectives while, at the same time, striving to set new ones.

When riders and other athletes begin to look forward, optimism suddenly takes a hand. We encourage people to start by setting goals that have intrinsic rewards, because these tend to be the best long-term motivators. Conversely, Olympic competitors often retire from sport because they forget to reset their goals, and thus lose their motivation. There is a continual stream of high-performance people who experience premature 'burnout' in riding. Their first experiences as riders are enjoyable because they meet their objectives – an important reward in itself. Over time, though, these same riders begin to focus solely on performance results, rather than enjoying the development of their ability for its own sake. The same phenomenon can occur with recreational riders. They begin taking lessons with the intention of eventually buying a horse and hacking out in the fresh air. As the lessons begin, a lot of hard work is involved in order to acquire the necessary skills. The rider and trainer become absorbed in exercises to develop these skills, and sometimes lose sight of the initial goal: pleasure. Somewhere along the journey both groups, the talented and the simply keen, lose sight of enjoyment, and their pursuits become drudgery.

Task 5. Just for fun, take a few moments to reflect on how your riding goals have evolved from your first experience to the present. Ask yourself whether you have met your objectives and retained your love of riding. Then chart the evolution of your riding goals on Figure 1 below.

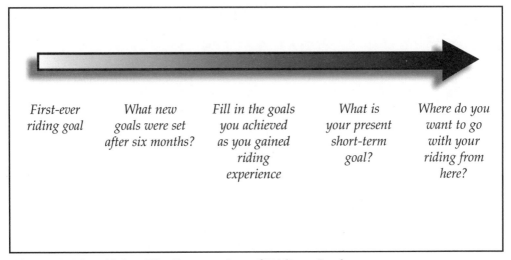

First-ever riding goal   *What new goals were set after six months?*   *Fill in the goals you achieved as you gained riding experience*   *What is your present short-term goal?*   *Where do you want to go with your riding from here?*

Figure 1: Identifying The Progression of Riding Goals

THE RECREATIONAL RIDER'S GOAL DIRECTION

Recreational riders of all ages select this sport for many reasons. They seem to share a love of nature, animals, and the solitude of a ride in the country. Most enjoy the physical exercise and body toning they receive from their riding. Their main goals seem to be the attainment of control and basic competence, so that they can pursue their chosen form of recreation. They take lessons to achieve these goals. Some wish to learn the finer points of dressage or jumping, but continue mainly for the pure pleasure of riding. An additional bonus is the camaraderie of like-minded people, who enjoy the post-ride coffee and chat about the horse, the ride and the achievements gained during the lesson. There is a pride in having stretched their capabilities and perhaps having overcome a fear. The goal, then, encompasses the physical, emotional, psychological and even the spiritual facets of the individual who has chosen this sport as a form of relaxation and recreation.

Most enjoy the physical exercise and body toning they receive from their riding.

THE COMPETITOR'S GOAL DIRECTION

Despite the importance of goals which are their own reward, reality dictates that some of our performances in life will be evaluated on outcome. For the competitor, results are one means of evaluating their training procedures in relation to other peoples'. Interestingly, however, if you were to ask a handful of riders at a competition what their performance goals were, some would say that they were competing for the fun of it, and others would look you unflinchingly in the eye, and say that they were trying to win. Both aims have their place in competitive riding. The rider who competes for fun achieves this goal by spending the weekend at a show enjoying the surroundings and the company of other enthusiasts. Top-level competitors, however, often have a different, more complex orientation; their competitive endeavours are directed concurrently by both the continued pursuit of excellence and by performance results.

PROCESS-DIRECTED GOALS FOR ALL RIDERS

As part of our human nature, we assess most of our long- and short-term objectives on the basis of concrete results. This includes comparing our abilities to others, as well as the attainment of rosettes and trophies. However, there is another very important method of evaluating performance. Life is a journey and a continuous learning experience, and riding is part of this valuable lesson. Riding progression and accomplishments are often explained by enjoyment alone. At times, we all let go of our expectations and ride simply for the pleasure of it. In so doing, we move forward because we want to experience more enjoyment, and this becomes the focus. As a result, our minds relax, our bodies soften and learning is inevitable. In this frame of mind, some of us might want to experiment with higher level dressage movements such as piaffe and passage. Others may focus on becoming more proficient in their show jumping skills. Because, in this instance, the fundamental goal is to partake of the process, that goal is readily achieved – it only requires a keen rider, an encouraging trainer, and a willing mount.

Task 6. Every rider, regardless of level, ought to have a plan they wish to follow from the moment of mounting onwards. The objective of each workout should be to bring the horse and rider partnership one step closer to the goals desired. Do you have a distinct programme to work through in order to attain your eventual long-term goal? After some reflection, identify the processes by which you intend to attain your goals. The skills to be addressed might vary from riding a straight line in the arena to working on Grand Prix dressage movements.

OUTCOME-BASED GOALS FOR TOP-LEVEL COMPETITORS

When it comes to top-level performance, result-directed goals can become helpful. All too often, we have seen riders base their performance goals on results that would be either obtainable without effort, or unattainable even with best-ever showings. The true purpose of performance-directed goals is to help competitors strive for difficult yet obtainable results. Experience has shown that, when competing at top level, it is easy to make the fundamental error of setting outcome goals too low: when doing so, one rarely performs to one's potential. Let us now share with you a very interesting and thought-provoking personal recollection of how result-directed goals can affect performance.

Case study

One year, in the not-too-distant past, Robert and two stable mates were preparing to leave for the Continental Young Rider's Championship – each to represent a different country and region. Beverley sat all three riders down and asked whether they would consider predicting their placings in the forthcoming competition. One of the girls explained that she feared the cross-country phase and so aspired merely to complete that phase, and the competition. The second rider felt that a top ten placing was realistic for her, and that was exactly where she set her sights. Robert was a little more ambitious. He wanted to finish in the top five. You will never guess what happened next. The girl who hoped to complete the competition did exactly that, and finished a respectable twenty-first out of approximately thirty finishers. The rider who hoped to finish in the top ten was pleased with her performance as well – probably because she finished in exactly tenth place. As for Robert, he finished in fifth place; no better, no worse.

HOW TO ACHIEVE REALISTIC, YET CHALLENGING GOALS

From the above experience one fundamental lesson was learned: we, as performers, can only go as far as the goals we set ourselves. When working with riders, whatever their aspirations, we help them to establish and re-evaluate goals that are realistic yet challenging. Initially, we might ask them to close their eyes and imagine themselves fulfilling their dearest ambitions. Before long, each person will be smiling, hoping, daring to dream of achievements that they would have earlier declared unattainable. Goal-setting, however, is part of the journey, not the destination and to move forward in this challenging trip, we need to establish our goals with due care and consideration.

Long-term goals are established as the first step of the procedure. For instance, a novice adult rider might have the long-term goal of becoming a basic-level competitive dressage rider. Short-term goals should always be compatible with your long-term vision, and help direct your progress toward the eventual objectives. Thus, the rider in our example would set a series of short-term goals based on issues such as obtaining an independent seat, learning the principles of applying the aids, learning how to achieve rhythmic movement in each gait, and so on.

Task 7. Based on the long-term goal you identified in Task 5, identify a series of short-term goals which lead step-by-step toward your long-term objective.

Last month's goals achieved:

This month's goals being worked on:

Next month's target goals:

Note that each of these short-term goals is part of an incremental progression toward your long-term objective. As each short-term goal is met, continue setting new and exciting goals, because this exercise is an ongoing process.

HOW TO SET GOALS THAT ENHANCE PERFORMANCE

Although we have discussed some of the principles related to goal-setting, there is more to this process than might be thought. While a long-term vision is a good reference point in any goal-setting process, this alone is not enough to ensure success. Many times, when people are asked to set themselves goals, one of two things happens: they set either challenging but generalized long-term objectives, or obvious targets that are attainable without much difficulty. However, in order for goals to promote best-ever performances, they need to be both challenging and specific. Therefore, we should take time to explore these options and evaluate the consequences of each.

1. More often than not, people choose goals that are both difficult and general in nature. The consequences of this choice provide much insight as to why many of us tend to lose some of our motivation. Those who make such a choice might aspire to become 'the best rider I can become'. When asked what it takes to meet such an objective, some find it difficult to specify criteria against which they can evaluate their abilities. Although many people aspire to progress in their own way, they become disconcerted once they start to realize that there is no method by which they can evaluate their development and feel pleased with their progress. Thus they will either lose interest in their riding pursuits or, hopefully, consult a knowledgeable trainer with whom they eventually map out a more specific and exciting course of action.

2. Other riders like to identify goals that are specific, yet easily attainable. A prime example of such a goal would be for a top show jumper to decide to ride a flawless and conservative round in a Grand Prix when they actually had the ability and a better-than-average chance to perform a fast clear round. Admittedly, goals that are simple and specific are better than no goals at all, but most people tend to sell themselves short when they adopt a goal that is too easy for their level of ability.

Other riders like to identify goals that are specific, yet easily attainable.

3. The best strategy for a rider of any level is to select a goal that is both challenging and specific. Examples of this form of goal-setting could be: focusing on a specific outcome such as a flawless show jumping round; a specific tactic in dealing with a tricky combination on the cross-country course; a certain quality of movement in a dressage test, or even a specific placing at a competition. The extent to which each of such aims is attained serves as a positive indicator upon

which to reset future goals. The one thing we like to tell people is to stretch their ambitions slightly out of reach so that they experience some 'growing pains'. After all, what people do not dream, they will never achieve. In 1996, much time was devoted to working with Olympic and Para-Olympic team candidates. As the athletes sat down to discuss their aims and intentions, many recognized that their goals were far too easy, and attempted to reset them to increase the level of challenge.

Setting difficult goals is risky, but undermining your potential is debilitating. Below is a summary of the criteria which will help you to establish or revise your goal-setting procedures.

CRITERIA TO ENSURE CORRECT LONG- AND SHORT-TERM GOAL-SETTING

- Long-term goals should be established under the guidance of a professional, enthusiastic trainer. You should take into account such factors as your access to suitable horses and training facilities and constraints of time and money. This will ensure that the goals established are specific and realistic; challenging, yet attainable.
- Once a solid long-term direction has been established, short-term evaluations are necessary to keep you moving towards your long-term goals. Achieving each short-term goal should bring you closer to the desired long-term objectives.
- Once long-term goals have been achieved, they should be revised to ensure continued motivation and direction.

PUTTING GOAL-SETTING INTO ACTION

We all set goals for ourselves daily. Some are long-term goals, others are revised each day. The question is, do we follow through with our ambitions and take the necessary measures to achieve them? The first step of this process involves identifying what we need to do in order to come closer to each one. Part of the progression includes becoming aware of our inner feelings and emotional struggles, and then establishing tactics to strengthen ourselves for the challenges that lie ahead.

Task 8. Now that you have reviewed the basic principles behind goal-setting, take your 'future goal' from Task 5, and write it down. Remember to select a goal that is both challenging and specific. Next, create four positive statements that would help you achieve your goal.

For instance, if you are an aspiring eventer but fear cross-country obstacles, you might want to set the goal of becoming an aggressive and talented cross-country rider. Each statement should then focus on one aspect of progress towards your goal, and thus become a positive affirmation. The statements might say: 'I am a strong and courageous rider', or 'I am a brave and confident rider'.

Task 9. Having completed your goal and affirmations, write them down on five or six index cards, starting with the goal at the top. Then place each index card somewhere you can see it a number of times daily. Each time you pass by the card, stop for one second and read the statements. Also, take the opportunity to actually imagine each goal at least once a day, and let yourself feel all the benefits and pride you will experience upon attaining the objective. These exercises will serve as reminders of where you are going, and will help you to focus on getting there.

Case Study

A few years ago, we were given the responsibility of managing a competitors' training programme for talented Young Riders. Their levels varied: some were representing their countries, others were being introduced to competition for the first time. During the first week of the programme we all sat together and shared aspirations for the coming season, as well as long-term goals. Amongst the group were two shy and timid riders, who feared jumping and competition. Nonetheless, they desired to stretch their limits; to compete, and jump small courses. When the two riders shared their goals with the other members of the group, they were supported and encouraged. Because the two were the best of friends, we encouraged them to develop shared affirmations. Referring to their goals, they decided they had to conquer their fears, and so they wrote on their index cards 'We are the combat twins', 'We are courageous', and 'We always persevere'. They posted their index cards in the washroom, by their saddles, on the doors of their horses' stables, by their beds, and everywhere else they visited frequently during each day. Within two weeks, these two riders were jumping complete courses, and shortly after, began to win every competition they were challenged with.

Having worked with those two riders, we now realize that a debt of gratitude is owed to them. Both former students and teaching staff alike knew that, in order to progress, we had to set goals that challenged us as individuals. However, none of us was consciously aware of how important it is to confront and overcome our fears in order to move forward until the 'combat twins' showed us the way as they conquered their own fear. During quests, it is perfectly normal to fear the difficult challenges that face us. However, some people turn their back on their fear and, in so doing, thwart their potential as performers and individuals. Those who succeed in their endeavours know that fear of the unknown can only be overcome by facing it and working through it. *Riding can become an opportunity to question our capabilities and extend our limits. However, before and whilst doing so, remember to request the advice of a knowledgeable, qualified trainer so that you meet your challenges on an appropriate step-by-step basis.*

Up to now, we have discussed the importance of imagery and goal-setting. Both components will play a central role in your pursuit of enjoyment and excellence. Imagery provides a positive picture, and a sense of familiarity with your riding and life objectives. We discussed it before goal-setting because our future visions often begin as fleeting thoughts which take the form of day-dreams. Once our dreams become objectives, they are stated as goals, both for the long and short term. Thus our visions are a positive starting point for improved performance – but only that. Once goals have been identified, we plan journeys that lead us towards our intentions. Doing this requires clearly directed focus and concentration. Therefore, the next chapter will explain how to develop focusing and concentration skills.

REMINDERS ON GOAL-SETTING

- Start with a long-term vision.
- Make certain that your long-term goals are both challenging and specific.
- Be sure to include process-directed goals along with the outcome goals that you set.
- Set, and adhere to, compatible short-term goals that will facilitate your long-term vision.
- Once your long-term goal is achieved, be sure to reset your goals to sustain motivation.

FURTHER READING

Burton, D. ' Goal setting in sport', in R.N. Singer, M. Murphey, and L.K. Tennant (eds.), *Handbook of research on sport psychology*, (New York, Macmillan 1993), pp.467-91.

Duda, J. L. 'Goals: A social cognitive approach to the study of achievement motivation in sport', in R. N. Singer, M. Murphey, and L. K. Tennant (eds.), *Handbook of research on sport psychology*, (New York, Macmillan 1993), pp.421-36.

Orlick, T. ' Targets and goals', *Psyching for sport*, (Champaign, Illinois, Human Kinetics 1986), pp.5-18.

Schinke, R. J. ' It's time to pursue those goals', *International Eventing*, vol. 2, (1996), pp. 50-1.

CHAPTER 4
FOCUSED
CONCENTRATION

Whatever the struggle continue to climb
it may be only one step to the summit.
Diane Westlake

Having set some specific riding goals for yourself, your next logical step is to develop and enhance your ability to focus positively upon daily and future objectives. Although it might sound easy, remaining focused on our endeavours presents quite a challenge.

We can probably all recall times when we drove our cars or rode our horses while our minds were elsewhere.

When we look back, we can probably all recall times when we drove our cars or rode our horses while our thoughts were elsewhere. For example, how often have you ridden your horse out on a hack and, at the same time, let your mind drift over the day's events? While you were deep in thought, your horse continued onward and, before you knew it, you were back at the stable wondering where your riding time had gone. As a result, you probably did not have the opportunity to appreciate the scenery that surrounded you, nor did you tune into your riding companion – your horse.

Overlooking opportunities such as these inevitably detracts from the quality of our rides. After all, people cannot move toward their goals by meandering aimlessly in situations which require deliberate focus. Therefore, concentration is a necessary tool to enhance performance and thus ease our path toward our goals. Let us then examine how varying levels of concentration can either assist or detract from your riding objectives.

BASIC CONCENTRATION SKILLS FOR RIDING

At all levels, riding is a sport that teaches us to improve our concentration skills. As beginners, we remain cautious and alert around horses, partially because of their size and also because we are advised to. We are told to enjoy the companionship of our four-legged partners, but also reminded not to get too close to certain horses, in order to avoid being kicked, bitten or stepped on. These repeated warnings result in heightened awareness. Later, as we become more proficient riders, we experience repeated reminders that we cannot treat our four-legged partners too casually. Eventually, some of us opt to participate in the demanding equestrian disciplines. In each of these, it becomes apparent that well-developed concentration is required to ensure that we perform to the best of our ability – partly because our horses demand nothing less.

THE HORSE: OUR TUNED-IN PARTNER

The horse is, by nature, a very sensitive creature, with a unique and open approach to communicating his needs to the rider. We humans also communicate our feelings to our horses. Sometimes we have feelings that we are probably able to conceal from the rest of the world; even from ourselves. We may carry anger, concern, fear, perplexity, elation, or excitement onto our horses when we mount them. These are emotions that we may well have concealed from our peers and colleagues for at least a short time – maybe longer. Partly through the actions of the kinesthetic senses, horses are acutely aware of these emotions, and it is often such emotions that set the tone for each day's ride. Despite this, we have stringent expectations of our horses. Whenever we ride them we expect them to behave well, remain attentive, and be willing and supple partners, regardless of our personal mood and emotional state.

The horse also has strong expectations and, since horses cannot speak, these are relayed to us in action and behaviour alone. Just as a jealous human mate or young child requires absolute concentration and love, so the horse demands comparable complete attention. To perform at their best, horses need to feel understood, and attended to. In exchange for our undivided attention, our horses readily give of themselves but, whenever we are out of touch with our them, they become spooky, inattentive, and uncooperative. In short, they become similar to dance partners who wish they were dancing with more sensitive companions. After all, riding mirrors dancing. When one partner is not focused on the thoughts and feelings of the other, the dance becomes a stiff, forced exchange between two entities.   In essence, the ultimate goal of the horse–rider combination is a level of synchronization at which two entities become one, the whole being better than the sum of its parts.

Task 10. In order to improve our riding performances, we must develop a strong understanding of how to improve our focusing abilities, as well as those of our horses. During the first part of the following exercise, identify a pre-ride approach that has helped your partnership perform well in the past. This approach should include the aims and emotions you bring with you to the ride.

On the basis of your reflections, establish a general philosophy that you feel will improve your partnership's focusing abilities during forthcoming rides, and then try it. Afterwards, make feedback notes detailing those components of the riding strategy that worked well, and also those that require refinement.

COMMON FOCUSING WEAKNESSES

At all levels, there are differences in the commitment that individual riders have to focusing on their objectives. Some set goals for themselves and, no matter what, will continue towards them. In order to move closer to their dreams, they will ignore any form of distraction or negativity. Others are never truly focused, either because they have forgotten to set goals for themselves, or have chosen not to do so. Either way, these riders have not established a direction upon which to concentrate.

There are other riders whose thoughts are often scattered and, as a consequence, they forget their initial objectives. In many cases, this group require more practice at filtering out extraneous thoughts and distractions whilst training and competing. One rider we worked with used to devote his attention to his school work and family whilst riding his horse then, when in school, would let his thoughts centre on his horse or family. As a result, he was rarely tuned in to his mount, or to his school classes. Slowly but surely, the horse began to withhold his talent until, eventually, his abilities were completely masked by anger, frustration and a reluctance to co-operate. On a happier note, however, we have also worked with riders who cultivated special relationships with their horses and, as a result, experienced meteoric climbs to the highest level of competition – The Olympic Games.

Case Study

In our experiences as trainers and sport psychologists, we have seen students applying many different focuses during their pursuit of riding excellence. This story concerns a former national team rider who provided a strong example of positive focus and commitment. The first time we saw her, as a ten-year-old girl, she was galloping by uncontrollably on a nasty pony; it appeared that she had been run away with. When we were introduced to her, we realized that there was something special about her. Although, just moments before, she had been terrorized by her pony, she was already planning how to get him under control in order to improve her performance for the next competition.

Three years later, she came to our doorstep for some training and competition experience. At the age of thirteen, she wasn't shy about saying that she was preparing for top-level competition – that was her focus. The following year, she returned for more schooling. Her thirst for winning motivated her to ride and care for her horses more than anyone we had ever met. Where many teenagers become side-tracked by their social lives, there was no deterring this rider. That year, she became the National Young Rider's Champion on a horse whom many qualified people had believed was an unpromising prospect. However, this talented Young Rider believed in herself and her horse and, as a result, the partnership began to exceed everyone's expectations. To cut a long story short, at the age of eighteen, this young lady became a member of her first Olympic Team, on the same horse.

Reflecting back on her progress up the competitive ladder, there is no question that this competitor was a talented rider even as a child. However, her ability to focus daily on her goal of becoming an Olympic rider, coupled with her resolution, patience, and belief in herself and her horse, was really what made her special.

All the qualities displayed by the rider in the case study above are important if we are to meet our objectives as riders. However, this chapter is primarly concerned with establishing and maintaining a focus, so let us now look at ways to improve concentration levels and focusing skills.

HOW TO IMPROVE YOUR CONCENTRATION SKILLS

Many riders and athletes believe that their best performances occur by chance. Often, we are introduced to national team members who believe that, on a good day, nothing can detract them from their aim. Conversely, we have all heard stories of world-class performers who were unshakeable during almost every competition they entered. These people became completely absorbed in their routines, to the extent where nothing existed for them during their performance but themselves and their horses. When each of us reflects on our own past experiences, we will undoubtedly recall times when we have experienced complete absorption in our actions. As with a child learning to play with a new toy, there are occasions when we completely lose track of time. Therefore, every one of us has the same ability to focus as the child or the consistent world-class performer – it is just a matter of knowing what we have to do in order to reach our most absorbed state.

When working with high-performance athletes on improving their concentration skills, we always ask them to recall recent experiences where they have been at their most focused. We then have them associate such occurrences with specific emotions and preparatory strategies, so that they can begin recalling their focus at will. The intention of the following exercise is to help you employ these same skills.

Task 11. Take a few minutes to identify one time in the recent past when you became completely absorbed in your activity. Once you have identified such a scenario, note the type of activity, and the frame

of mind you were in at the time. Also, make a rough estimate of the time for which you were completely absorbed in your task.

Just as there are distinct behaviours and moods that can be associated with a focused state, there are also those that can be associated with a lack of focus – being 'diffused', or 'scattered'. Some riders, for instance, become scattered when they are over-anxious before testing their abilities. Because of this, we often ask riders to identify situations, emotions and moods that occur prior to, and during, unfocused performances. The information they compile thus highlights emotional and behavioural areas that should be avoided before and during those times when they need to be at their best.

Task 12. Take a few minutes to identify one time in the recent past where your focus was scattered during a riding-related activity. Once you have identified such a scenario, note what sort of activity and mood state you were in at the time. Also, reflect and identify the emotions that occurred prior to and during this difficult ride.

Now that you have identified how your own concentrated and diffused focuses occur, as well as how they feel, it is time to discuss the importance of how a negative focus begins, and how it can be changed into a positive perspective.

WORKING THROUGH FOCUSING CHALLENGES

Everyone, from the beginner to the most disciplined and accomplished performer, experiences challenges in establishing or regaining focus from time to time. The question often comes down to how capable we are of coping with our loss of attention. Some people, whether riding recreationally, during training, or in competition, experience a 'downward spiral' – when a momentary decrease in concentration begins a chain of events that cause a performance to deteriorate far below its potential. Such a scenario might begin with a rider warming up for a dressage competition. Just as the horse and rider are beginning to settle into their routine, an unknowledgeable spectator walking by opens an umbrella. Within a split second, the rider becomes side-tracked by the spectator's mistake and consequently focuses energy in the form of anger towards the spectator. Affected by actions totally beyond personal control, the rider has become uptight and flustered, and the horse reacts by shying away from the umbrella and his rider's anger. At that specific moment, the rider comes to a crossroad with the horse, and might opt to scold him, instead of recalling previously learned focusing strategies, and regrouping. The horse becomes increasingly upset, the rider grows angrier by the moment, and what promised to be a peak performance deteriorates into a sub-standard result.

However, trying situations do not necessarily have to detract from the quality of performance. In fact, many world-class performers in all sports view adversity as a test of themselves, which they have the ability to overcome despite the odds. Therefore, such challenges can be motivating and, if viewed as obstacles that can be overcome, may even culminate in best-ever results. When challenges to focusing are viewed positively, they become the start of an 'upward spiral'. For example, a horse might begin a dressage warm-up more alert than usual and, as a result, appear spooky. At that moment, the rider can begin taking advantage of the horse's new-found energy, and channel it to produce a more energetic, brilliant, and synchronized performance, with an abundance of impulsion.

Having reflecting on our personal strengths and weaknesses in focusing, it becomes evident that we have the power to choose how and when to focus and channel our energies. The options teeter, however, between a positive or negative emphasis and, at the same time, there is also the matter of either partial or complete attention. In order to maintain a positive and complete focus, and thus achieve improved results, what we have to do is call on a strategy that works best for us. Doing so requires an intentional effort, which some sport psychologists call 'deliberate attention'.

RIDING WITH DELIBERATE ATTENTION

As with other skills, improving concentration requires a concerted effort, and the focus of each effort will vary according to the day's riding objective. Sometimes, riding is used to achieve rest and relaxation. In such cases, especially with people working under stress, the focus is upon enjoying the countryside and getting away from the office. In a different context, such as a schooling environment, the objective of the ride may be to improve a specific riding skill under the guidance of an expert trainer. Both forms of riding, and any other you might suggest, require the same deliberately focused attention in order to achieve their aims.

The method for improving your deliberate attention is quite simple – it merely requires your commitment to its aim. Just before each ride, set a distinct goal for the ride. For the first few times, we recommend that you write your goal on a small piece of paper, and place it in a pocket that is easily accessible during your ride. Next, take a few moments to recall which emotions and perspectives you have employed during enjoyable rides in the past. If you cannot recall the specifics, refer back to Task 11. Once you have an objective for your ride, mount up, and remain committed to the goal you have just set yourself. If, at any time, you begin to lose sight of your objective, pull out the piece of paper with your stated goal, take a moment to visualize it, then allow the image to redirect you towards your objective.

Task 13. When you have completed your ride, work through the following questionnaire. It will help you to improve your next ride by providing you with a greater awareness of what you did correctly, as well as some hints on procedures to avoid in the future.

1. What was your goal for the ride?

2. Were you able to maintain your goal throughout the ride?

3. Were you able to replicate positive emotions and memories of a previous enjoyable ride?

4. Were you able to maintain your optimal state of mind and focus for at least parts of the ride? If so, for how long?

5. Were there significant differences in the quality of your performance when you were in your optimal state of mind, as compared to other moments? If so, identify these differences.

6. Were there times where your focus was scattered? If so, explain what happened just prior to and during this part of your ride.

7. Is there something you will revise in your focusing strategy to improve your next ride? In so doing, you will be setting a new focus.

RE-FOCUSING THROUGH SELF-TALK

Focusing strategies are central to improving riding. At the same time, postive re-focusing tactics can be developed to enhance performance. Often, turning a difficult circumstance around in a positive way requires nothing more than some common sense and a few easily learnt methods.

On many occasions we lose our focus, and become frustrated by our inability to re-focus. As a result, we often put ourselves through negative forms of self-talk such as 'I give up', 'Forget it', 'I just can't do this', 'Why am I here?' or 'It's hopeless'. This sort of self-talk is debilitating, and only serves to detract from one's goals, both in riding and life in general: in short, it contributes to the downward spiral discussed earlier. In order to re-establish an upward spiral, we can use positive words to empower our performances.

Task 14. Next time you ride, experiment with the use of positive self-talk. Try riding your horse effectively whilst thinking of words and phrases with positive connotations: 'exceptional', 'good job', or' way to go'. Notice how your muscles, body posture, and emotions are affected positively as you employ such positive words. After employing this strategy on a ride, evaluate your performance using the following criteria:
Mood state:

Confidence:

Muscle flexibility:

Riding to potential:

Enjoyment of the ride and your horse:

Meeting your objectives:

Motivation for next ride:

To summarize, use of positive words or phrases can help you in one of two ways: they can either help set the tone for a performance, or help you re-focus in any riding context. When setting the tone for each ride, remember to review the positive affirmations you wrote on index cards for Tasks 6 and 7. When re-focusing, athletes who have been successful with verbal reminders have found that concentration is established, or returns, almost immediately after their use. Remember, however, that as with all skills, self-talk requires regular practice in order to be at its most effective.

TRAINING WITH POTENTIAL DISTRACTIONS

Many competitors across the sporting spectrum develop re-focusing plans aimed at coping with distractions and retaining attention. This can be achieved by developing a list of potential distractions that might occur at future competitions, and then formulating plans for coping with each. For instance, a dressage rider might ask someone on the ground to open and close an umbrella during general schooling and test rehearsals. Other simulated distractions might include having a dog run inside the arena, or someone dropping pieces of paper during practice on a windy day. For a recreational rider, distractions might include riding in an arena with as many other riders as possible, or employing the use of strange noises.

For a recreational rider, distractions might include employing the use of strange noises.

Practice of this sort serves as a test of your ability to remain focused on your riding goals, and also develops a sense of confidence in your ability to cope with distractions.

For competition riders, many of the distractions that can be added into pre-season schooling might be deemed as mirroring normality. One of the more obvious would be shortening the length of your warm-up by twenty minutes as if you had arrived late at a horse show! Those of you who are dressage riders and eventers might have someone imitating an irritable tack steward, checking your equipment before you enter the arena immediately prior to a test rehearsal. For the show jumping discipline, you might want to practise your jumping warm-up while all the fences are being continually vied for by others. Each rider in each discipline will have some particular ways of testing and improving focusing skills. In short, it is just a matter of identifying which distractions are applicable to you, your horse, and the constraints under which you compete.

Ideally, re-focusing strategies should be practised regularly on your home ground before the start of each season. Initially, they should be practised throughout winter schooling in the comfort of your own yard: later, for those who are competitors, they should be integrated into competition dress rehearsals. This procedure will help to ensure that you develop an automatic response to coping with distractions, regardless of your chosen discipline. The three tasks that follow will help you to establish coping procedures to suit your own circumstances.

Task 15. Take a few minutes to identify and note down some distractions that have bothered you in the past.

Task 16. Now that you have identified some distractions, identify procedures that would help you cope better with the four most prevelant ones.

Task 17. Having identified past distractions, and outlined a strategy for coping with them, select two and reproduce both in the security of your home stable. While doing so, ensure that you are under the supervision of your trainer, or under the scrutiny of an expert rider. After you have completed the ride, take a few moments to assess whether you remained focused throughout each distraction. Also, note details of how you can further improve your strategies for coping during your next attempts at this exercise.

Even though you have completed the distraction exercises for the first time, much work lies ahead. If the first attempt at distraction control proved weaker than you had hoped for, try it again until it works. Also, feel free to practise as many re-focusing scenarios around distractions as are necessary in order for you to feel confident about both your own and your horse's ability to maintain concentration. This ability can only develop through continued practice and lots of patience.

SUMMARIZING FOCUSING

During this chapter, we have covered a variety of focusing issues, solutions and exercises. The first part of the chapter centred on our general tendency to ride with varying levels of focus. We then looked at the fact that, just as we expect focused attention from our horses, so they demand the same undivided attention from us during every moment to perform as a team. When either one of the two partners becomes unfocused, the performance of both will inevitably suffer. Therefore, every focusing strategy discussed took both partners into account, with a view to improving the performance of the horse – rider combination as a whole.

The recommendations for improving focusing skills began with suggestions of how to combat negative situations and turn them into positive ones. Suggestions were then given as to how to improve focus step-by-step for recreational riding, training and competition. Concurrently, there was emphasis on the need to establish an awareness of how, when, and why we become unfocused during our rides. Following on from this, the final section of the chapter discussed how to train with distractions, and also emphasized the importance of positive self-talk as a means of refining our focusing skills.

Although the fact has only been alluded to thus far, our ability to concentrate also requires an optimal level of energy. Therefore, we need to establish the correct levels of relaxation and activation that work for us and our horses in the context of each riding discipline. If this aim is not achieved, one of two problems may occur. At one end of the spectrum, we (and our horses) will become over-activated and nervous: a heightened level of energy will result in our focus becoming diffused and scattered. Conversely, when over-relaxed, we will become sleepy and inattentive. The next chapter will address these issues in detail.

REMINDERS ON FOCUSING

- Focusing strategies are skills that need to be practised daily.
- Be sure to identify focusing tactics that enhance, rather than detract from, your performance.
- Remember that we all lose our focus at times. When this happens, there are specific re-focusing tools that you can call upon.
- Positive self-talk can be employed to re-affirm a positive focus.
- Self-talk and cue words can also be used as tools in times of adversity.
- Remember that focusing is essentially 'deliberate attention'.

FURTHER READING

Gendlin, E. T. *Focusing*, (London, Bantam 1982).

Kroll, W. ' The stress of high performance athletics', in P. Klavora and J. Daniels (eds.), *Coach, athlete, and the sport psychologist*, (Toronto, University of Toronto 1979), pp.211-20.

Orlick, T. ' Refocusing at the event', *Psyching for sport*, (Champaign, Illinois, Human Kinetics 1986), pp.59-70.

Schinke, R. J. ' Focusing and direction for equestrian performers', *Australian Horse & Rider*, vol. 9, (1995), pp.27-9.

Schinke, R. J. 'Decide your own destiny', *International Eventing*, vol. 1, (1996), pp. 50-1.

CHAPTER 5
RELAXATION-ACTIVATION FOR PEAK PERFORMANCE

Men cannot see their reflection in running water, but only in still water.
Confucius

Up to this point we have discussed the importance of imagining, setting and then focusing on our goals. However, phased progression – and even focusing for that matter – become difficult unless we establish an energy level that works best for us as riders. As we gain in experience, we learn that our bodies and minds (and those of our horses) function best at a specific energy level which relates to individual temperament and the demands of the discipline in question. In order to replicate top-quality performances, we first need to learn how to identify the energy level that works best, and then develop methods to reproduce it at will. As with the subjects already discussed, relaxation-activation is a component of our daily lives that can be built upon with a minimum of effort. The purpose of this chapter, therefore, is to explore how varying levels of energy affect our riding performance, and to explain how you can identify and maintain an energy level that will work best for you, regardless of your riding level and favoured discipline.

Most people, from the novice rider to the international performer, are unable to attain consistently an energy level that suits their temperaments. Indeed, some of the high-performance athletes with whom we work believe that luck – both good and bad – dictates the outcome of all their performances. They will argue that, when they perform at their best, they achieve a good result as part of a random process that entails being in the right place at the right time, and involves external factors beyond their control. However, the most consistent performers know their correct energy level, and have established a procedure in order to reproduce it at will. In essence, we are all capable of performing at our best regularly, provided that we approach each ride with the same positive attitude and energy level.

The question that lies before us then, is how we actually intend to establish and reproduce this optimum energy level. Before beginning to answer this question, let us first look at a little background theory of how personal activation levels tend to work with all living creatures.

There are many views regarding how optimum levels of activation are assessed. One popular model is the 'inverted U theory', which indicates 'the zone of optimal functioning'.

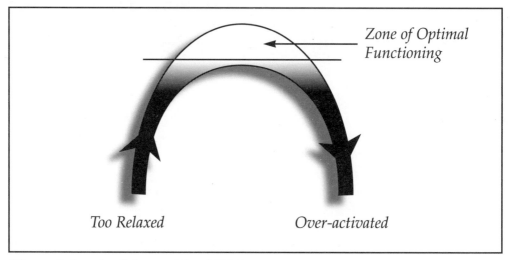

Figure 2: Levels of Arousal for Athletes

If you examine Figure 2, you will see that our levels of activation can vary between low and high energy states. At the peak, or mid-point of the inverted U, is the zone of optimal functioning – the optimal performance state. The implication of the diagram is fairly straightforward: our correct energy levels rest somewhere between two ends of a continuum. The left side of the diagram represents an over-relaxed, lethargic state. Some riders, both competitive and recreational, fall into this category. The opposite, extreme right end of the diagram, represents riders who become over-activated and, as a result, become either anxious and 'scattered', or else compensate through continual yawning. Somewhere in between these two states we each have an optimal performance state which is unique to ourselves. Some people will perform at their best when they are psyched up before a competition, whereas others require relaxation techniques in order to wind down, because otherwise their thinking loses focus.

Some people will perform at their best when they are psyched up before a competition.

ACTIVATION LEVELS IN RIDING

In the sport of riding, some of us react to riding-related stress by bouncing around and talking a mile a minute to anyone and everyone. Others are sleepy, and unaware of what is going on in their immediate environment. Although both groups of people are viewed as vastly different because of their differing coping mechanisms they are, in fact, attempting to cope with many of the same difficulties and are searching for many of the same answers. We cannot assume, therefore, that one method of reacting to stress and challenge is more common than the other. What we can agree on is that, since extreme levels of relaxation and activation detract from our performance in every aspect of our lives, they can be assumed to act as stumbling blocks in our pursuit of riding excellence.

Case Study

It is always interesting to watch riders in situations they find stressful. Some cope with their nerves by becoming sleepy. At the opposite end of the scale, you will find the 'fired up' rider, who has to do anything and everything before mounting. As a three-day event rider, Robert was the type who couldn't keep his eyes open before it was time to mount. He would sit in his hotel room, or even on the trunk outside his horse's stable, and doze in and out of consciousness before mounting to warm up for the cross-country. One team-mate, on the other hand, was highly strung and, when attempting to handle his pre-competition jitters, would speak at a speed too fast for anyone to follow. Although both riders were distinctly different in the way they coped with their energy, they shared a common pursuit: both were searching for an activation level from which they were energized enough to perform, yet relaxed enough to think clearly. It soon became obvious that the person who was better able to achieve the correct balance between energy and clear thinking tended to outperform the other.

It is unlikely that anyone has described the delicate balance between relaxation and activation more succinctly than Michael Plumb, the top American three-day event rider. He feels that, in order to give a best performance, a rider has to be 'on fire but thinking'. It is the quest for this delicate balance between two energy levels that we will now embark upon.

Task 18. Take a few moments to complete the questionnaire below. Its purpose is to help you identify and refine the activation levels that work best for you and your horse.

1. Do you ride each respective equestrian discipline with a consistent mood and energy level? Explain.

2. Was there a specific activation level associated with your best performances?

3. Was there a specific activation level associated with your horse's best performances?

4. What activation level has led to your own sub-standard performances in past rides?

5. What activation level has led to your horse's sub-standard performances in past rides?

6. Have you previously used any mental preparation strategies to
   establish the correct activation level for the relevant equestrian discipline? If so, which ones worked best?

7. If you were asked to design a riding strategy aimed at you and your
   horse reaching your optimal energy levels together, what would it
   include?

**Task 19. Once you have completed Task 18, study it carefully, then
design and write down a strategy for your next ride. The purpose of
this task is to facilitate the correct activation level for yourself, your
horse, and the intended exercise. Once the ride has been completed,
take a few minutes to answer the following questions.**

1. Were you and your horse able to perform at an energy level that was
   suitable for the two of you? Explain.

2. Identify parts of your ride that went correctly, and identify what
   frame of mind and which elements of the warm-up led to this.

3. Identify parts of your ride which could have been improved, and
   identify what frame of mind and riding tactics led to this.

ACHIEVING OPTIMAL
RELAXATION-ACTIVATION LEVELS

Up to this point, we have discussed the importance of identifying the
optimal activation levels for you and your horse. Now let us look at
some of the relaxation and activation exercises that can help you establish or re-create the correct energy level for consistently good performances. When reading this section, allocate fifteen minutes for each of
the next three days to practise at least one of the exercises.

SUGGESTIONS ON HOW TO RELAX

In this section, we will explore several of the relaxation exercises
employed by many of the top athletes from various sports with whom
we have worked. Although the proposed exercises have been used most

frequently by top-level performers, rest assured that they will work equally well for riders of all levels and equestrian disciplines. We only ask that you attempt each suggested exercise a number of times, since the improvement of your mental game-plan will require patience and perseverance.

Meditation

The first, and most popular form of relaxation exercise, is meditation. Meditation can be defined as any exercise that facilitates a clearing of the stresses from the mind and body – a definition that encompasses many different themes and methods. Ultimately, the goal of any such exercise is to produce a state of total calmness and relaxation. As with any other form of soothing activity, meditation requires much practice, and the approach adopted should always be tailored to the needs of the user. You might, for example, want a guided style of meditation, where you are taken on a 'journey' by a narrator. This type of meditation is discussed further in due course. Another option is to meditate without any external help, by developing your own relaxing image that you can employ whilst listening to soft music. There are many possible choices of images that may facilitate total relaxation. One option is a beautiful pastoral setting with a variety of trees, running water, green meadows, and birds. If such a setting is not to your liking, let your mind wander towards a warm and sunny ocean scene, where soft waves meet and pull away from the sand at your feet.

Multi-sensual images such as these are developed or reproduced through your mind's eye in what sport psychologists call your 'quiet place'. However, before developing this theme, it is necessary to provide a lead-in procedure that facilitates the necessary relaxed state. The simplest method for achieving relaxation is often termed 'deep abdominal breathing'.

Deep Abdominal Breathing (DAB)

As a lead-in to imagery, deep abdominal breathing establishes a sense of calm, whereby the mind is prepared for clear and positive thought in advance of the forthcoming meditation. However, it also has a second, distinct, use as an immediate relaxation exercise when mounted. Often, when riding, the activation levels of both the recreational rider and the top-level performer are affected by varying levels of oxygen intake. When people become overwhelmed and nervous, they unintentionally take in shallower breaths, and therefore reduced quantities of air. When this happens, the mental processes become scattered, and thoughts become negative or, at very least, unclear. At the same time, the body responds to the lack of oxygen with an increased sense of fatigue.

The following exercise provides a step-by-step explanation of how to perform deep abdominal breathing in both mounted and unmounted contexts.

If not mounted, begin by either sitting or lying down in a comfortable, stretched-out position. If mounted, bring your horse to a walk and then allow yourself to settle into the saddle. Next, slow down your thinking by remembering your 'quiet place' (see below). Then, breathe in gradually through your nose whilst counting to five; hold, also to the count of five, then exhale through your mouth. As you exhale, let go of any tension you might be carrying in your shoulders and ribcage. Be sure to breathe in, hold, and exhale a total of five times per exercise for maximum benefit. This whole procedure should probably take you no more than three minutes in total. Once the exercise is completed, take a moment to notice how strong and invigorated you feel for your forthcoming riding or imagery task. Also, try pairing it with at least one of the relaxation-imagery exercises which follow.

Your quiet place

This concept might, at first, sound somewhat abstract. However, we have received much positive feedback from people – including all levels of athletes and business professionals – regarding its usefulness. Ultimately, people have learned an effective way of achieving a state of relaxation within a five minute period. The reason why many high-level performers call on this exercise is that, with well-developed concentration skills, they can return to their quiet place regardless of the commotion that goes on around them. Thus there is much evidence to support the benefit of developing your own quiet place. All that is required is ten or fifteen minutes where you can be alone in a quiet corner. In order to develop your own personal quiet place, follow the steps proposed below.

Task 20. Allocate a few minutes to establish whether you can identify a relaxing, positive, mental image of something you have encountered in the past. Previously identified quiet places have included pastoral settings, ocean scenes, comfortable living rooms with crackling fireplaces, and places in the countryside that conjure up a sense of well-being. If a relaxing place does not come to mind, list the ingredients

that relax you, and develop your own imaginary quiet place. Make a note of the image you have identified.

Task 21. Now that you have identified your relaxing image, allocate five minutes to implement the imagery exercise with relaxing instrumental music. Be sure to lead into the exercise with some deep abdominal breathing. Once the exercise is completed, evaluate and note the results.

Guided meditation

As we have seen, meditation is simply a quietening exercise. Guided meditation (also called guided imagery), has the same aim, but also has directives. We allow our bodies to relax, we breathe slowly and deeply, and we clear our minds.

In order to prepare fully for this exercise, you need to find a quiet room where you will not be disturbed. Telephone bells should be turned off, lights dimmed, and the room should be warm and quiet. The twenty minutes or so that you are reserving for yourself must be planned so that you will be undisturbed. Thus you prepare a setting which promotes the full measure of relaxation.

You may find yourself with an itch, or having thoughts that intrude. That does not matter. Simply do whatever you need to do to be comfortable: scratch the itch; allow the thoughts to pass. It may take a few attempts before you can actually 'let go' of all the intrusion. This does take practice, and you will get the knack of it. Remember, this is a time for you to relax and release all tension; it is a well-deserved gift that you give to yourself.

Guided meditation has many principles similar to the quiet place previously discussed. For one, its objective is to place you in a quiet and comforting frame of mind, so that you have time to clear and compose your thoughts. In order to induce this state, all you have to do is follow a pre-formulated mental script that appeals to the senses. As with the self-guided quiet place, the images in this exercise should include elements of the natural world, such as the ocean, trees, grass, a light breeze, sun and warmth – or all of these ingredients at the same time. Once this mental script has been established, the next step is to identify a soothing piece of music that you find compatible with it. We recommend that, if you select an appropriate piece of soothing New Age music, it should include some natural sounds compatible with the mental images. For further references to guided meditation and imagery, you can refer to Chapters 2 and 8.

CUES AND TRIGGER WORDS FOR RELAXATION AND ACTIVATION

Most of the exercises discussed up until now are best employed dismounted. However, there are also several relaxation and activation exercises that can be implemented to help produce the correct energy level whilst riding. In the context of mounted exercises, we will be using words termed 'cues' in situations where relaxation is required and words termed 'triggers' in situations where increased activation is necessary. Both cues and triggers can be used to help you and your trainer identify or re-establish the appropriate relaxation-activation level for a forthcoming task. Let us now examine when and how to use these forms of self-talk.

Some people who are just beginning to ride become tense when they venture into open areas. Other people become nervous before jumping various sorts of obstacles. Such concerns are often attributed to the fear

THIS IS ONE HECK OF A SAND SCHOOL, BOY, BUT I GUESS WE'LL MAKE IT ACROSS THE LONG DIAGONAL.

Some people who are just beginning to ride become tense when they venture into open areas.

that they will lose control of their mounts. The following case study provides an example of how a cue word can be used to lower your activation level whilst raising your confidence level to a preferred state for jumping.

Case study

Marie came to us after competing in her first Pre-novice horse trial. She felt discouraged because every time she approached an obstacle with her horse, they would rush towards it. Together, we decided to experiment with some relaxation techniques within a lesson framework. First, we asked to see her jump a cross-pole from trot. As she began the approach, her body tensed, her breathing became shallow, and her horse began to increase speed. To solve this problem, Marie had to learn how to approach the obstacle in a relaxed, casual way. The exercise she was taught employed a five-stage process. First, we helped her to identify her nervousness as the root of the horse-rider problem, and then we searched for possible solutions. Second, she was asked to identify one cue word that described the strategy she needed in order to approach the fence in a relaxed state. 'Soft' was the word agreed upon as mean-ingful. Then, we asked Marie to begin riding towards the fence in trot. As she approached the obstacle the first three times, she could hear us saying 's.o.f.t.' in a very soothing and relaxed tone. As she continued over the obstacle, she was asked to concentrate on the tone of voice and the implication of the word being spoken. On the third attempt, her body seemed to soften before the fence, she began to breathe deeply and, as a result, her horse began to relax. Next, we asked Marie herself to say 's.o.f.t' out loud as she approached the fence. Through this process, she began to integrate her cue word. Her jumping remained relaxed over the cross-poles and then later over small verticals. Finally, Marie was told simply to think 's.o.f.t'. She was astonished to find that she and her horse continued to approach each fence in a soft and rhythmic way. The solution to her pre-jump nerves was simple: all she had to do was replace her nervous and rapid internal chatter with more helpful self-talk, and thereby improve her thought processes.

On the other hand, we have also witnessed times where both a horse and rider tended to perform on the under-activated, over-relaxed end of the scale. At such times, it is preferable to call on triggers rather than cues. The following case study concerns a horse – Young Rider partnership with whom we had the opportunity to work as they progressed from regional to national and then to international level in three-day eventing.

Case study

Even from the beginning, Peter and his horse were laid-back although, at the same time, very talented. Initially, at the lower levels of eventing, they made a very showy team, and were always in the ribbons without expending much effort. That, it seems, was the problem. As they progressed through the ranks up to FEI levels, they could no longer afford to coast – they needed to take a more pro-active approach to performance if they wanted continued success. But, as Peter and his horse progressed, their activation remained low and their results reflected this. Then, at one competition, Peter's trainer felt so frustrated that he pinched the rider to wake him up, prior to his leaving the start box. That particular pinch did the trick: the startled rider woke up, had a brilliant cross-country ride, and finished well placed. In retrospect, we can see that Peter could have awoken and activated himself had he developed a trigger word or phrase that energized him – like 'go for it' or 'let's go'.

It is always satisfying to have solutions as simple as the ones we have just described. As soon as a problem is identified and acknowledged, remedies are actually quite easy to find. Regardless of whether your shortcoming is jumping sizeable fences, galloping fast, performing in front of a large audience, or mounting a certain horse for the first time, the word exercises described above will work for you. Remember though, to choose a cue or trigger word that is both meaningful to you and consistent with what you want to achieve, and to implement it in a suitable tone. Remember, also, that there is a preferred sequence for integrating the self-talk phrase into your consciousness. It is helpful to begin the exercise with someone else calling out the cue or trigger, so that you actually hear the appropriate tone while you first address your objective. Then, you can begin to integrate the cue word into your self-talk first by saying it out loud, and then by saying and thinking it internally.

Now that we have discussed some applications of positive cue and trigger words, it is time to try out the exercise on yourself or, if you are a trainer, to implement the exercise with one of your students.

Task 22. Take a few moments to identify a situation that either over- or under-activates you. Once you have identified a specific situation that detracts from your optimal energy level, search for a cue or trigger word that represents the mental state you are seeking. Remember that it must be said in the correct tone to connect you with the energy level you require. When you are ready, mount your horse and, under supervision from your trainer, gradually begin to undertake the challenge, following the three-step process outlined above. After experimenting with your cue or trigger word, assess the results as outlined below.

Word identified:

How soon was implementation successful when word spoken by external source? Possible reasons why:

How soon was implementation successful when word was spoken personally?

How successful was implementation when word was repeated mentally?

These word selection exercises and various forms of imagery are extremely helpful when you have half an hour or so to allocate to them. However, there are times when performers need more immediate 'quick fixes' with which to regulate their activation levels. Therefore, on the basis of our past experience of working with international competitors, we have produced solutions that can work in the short term. The alpha state exercise described below is one example that continues to serve people well – including some of Canada's 1996 Olympic athletes.

RETURNING TO THE ALPHA STATE

Reflect for a moment on what it feels like when you experience a deep sleep. As you do so, you will most certainly identify the difference between a deep sleep and one that is fitful. During the times when we progress through our sleep, and enter into a deeper state of relaxation, our eyes tend to roll upward and, as a result, our bodies soften. Although this complete state of relaxation does not assist you as a performer, there are times when parts of this relaxation experience could prove beneficial. The Task that follows provides an instaneous relaxation technique that induces what is known as the 'alpha experience'. For most people, this exercise is sufficient to provide a discernible improvement in relaxation. Furthermore, as with deep breathing and self-talk, it can be employed both while you are mounted and dismounted. Try it!

Task 23. Take three deep breaths as described in the section on deep breathing (DAB). Whilst keeping your head straight, move your eyes slowly to look upward as much as possible. Initially, you will feel a slight amount of discomfort. However, continue the exercise until you feel your eyelids becoming heavy. Usually this happens after 10–15 seconds. Then, very slowly, let your eyelids close while you are taking another deep breath. Let your mind and body soften to the experience. Once you have completed the exercise, take a few moments to note the body and mind sensations that have resulted. Was there a notable difference in your relaxation level?

This is an exercise that requires practice and patience to perfect. We assure you, though, that when you practise it over time, the alpha exercise will facilitate an almost instant relaxation.

SUMMARIZING RELAXATION AND ACTIVATION

This chapter has introduced a number of different terms and concepts, which may be somewhat bewildering initially. It may be that you want to become comfortable with the relaxation techniques before you proceed further. Once you have learned to relax totally, you can try other guided meditations. Some will activate you; some will have a quietening effect. You are free to select whatever is appropriate to your needs at any given time. Should you choose to practise the guided imageries, it will become increasingly easy to capture the feeling you are seeking. Only you will know which cues and triggers work best for you, and which relaxation and activation exercises serve you well. With practice, you will become more proficient at implementing each of the exercises to achieve the desired state.

Beyond the traditional benefits that relaxation offers, another bonus you will gain is the effect your new responses have on those around you. We have noticed that some athletes and trainers stimulate each other unconsciously and sometimes unnecessarily, creating either too much or too little energy. This may hamper rather than enhance a performance. However, athletes who learn to control their own levels of activation often influence the activation levels of those around them. Specifically, the energy levels of the rider, trainer, family member or friend are no longer diffused or inappropriate, so everybody is free to do their job to the best of their ability.

During this chapter, we have provided some specific suggestions on how to establish the correct activation-relaxation level but, even when you employ these ideas, there will be times when you will feel a decline in your performance level. This phenomenon, which is common to everyone, will be discussed in the next chapter.

REMINDERS ON RELAXATION AND ACTIVATION

- Optimal levels of relaxation and activation vary from person to person.
- Repetition of all exercises, both on and off the horse, can only be beneficial.
- Make sure to practise at least one exercise from both the 'quick fix' and longer-term suggestions twice a week.
- All athletes involve themselves in some form of internal monologue. For best results, select appropriate cues or triggers to help produce the correct level of energy.

FURTHER READING

Butt, S. D. ' Treatment techniques', *Psychology of sport*, (New York, Van Nostrand Reinhold 1987), pp.182-94.

Lynch, J. ' Relaxation', *Thinking body, dancing mind: Tao sports for extraordinary performance in business, sport and life*, (New York, Bantam 1992), pp.46-52.

Nideffer, R. ' Attention control training', in R. N. Singer, M. Murphey, and L. K. Tennant (eds.), *Handbook of research on sport psychology*, (New York, Macmillan 1993), pp.542-56.

Schinke, R. J. ' Establishing the optimal level of relaxation-activation for peak performances', *Australian Horse & Rider*, vol. 8, (1995), pp. 26-28.

CHAPTER 6
PEAKS, VALLEYS AND PLATEAUX

The courage of working for
something you believe in,
day in and day out, year after year,
can be difficult but holds the greatest rewards.
V. Sukomlin

Up until now, each chapter has addressed a specific strategy designed to improve performance. It is, however, an inescapable fact that all athletes, including riders, experience progress, setbacks and times when their development seems to stand still. Sometimes, the factors that create stumbling blocks or inconsistencies are potentially unavoidable. At other times, they will inevitably continue for a while, but can be better coped with if the reasons behind them are better understood. The purpose of this chapter is, then, to explore and de-mystify the phenomena we term peaks, valleys and plateaux.

DEFINING PEAKS, VALLEYS AND PLATEAUX

Each one of us, as riders, has undoubtedly experienced a mixture of ups and downs, and periods of stagnation, which we can define as peaks, valleys and plateaux. Peaks, undoubtedly, are instances where we and our horses feel as one. During such times, we no longer think deliberately about what we are doing. Instead, we let our bodies take over and meld with our horses. The eventer going across country, for instance, may experience a flow during which obstacles are taken effortlessly, as incidental parts of the horse's galloping strides. Interestingly, when we are asked to recapture such experiences, we often have difficulty describing the details, because we have ridden by feel and reflex. Conversely, during valleys, we become entirely separate entities, out of harmony with our horses. In the midst of such experiences, we usually

Peaks, undoubtedly, are instances where we and our horses feel as one.

begin to try hard to think of what is required to complete the necessary task. As a result, our bodies become mechanical, and our aids become unsynchronized, stiff and forced. In show jumping, for example, the horse may fight the rider on the approach to an obstacle and, because of the resistance of the rider's signals, will jump the fence off a bad stride, with the rider out of balance and harmony. Plateaux are those times when we experience no progress in our skills – or so we sense. For a dressage rider, an example of a plateau would be when similar comments and scores are received from several judges throughout the whole show season. During times such as these, we perceive ourselves as stale, and therefore we lose motivation.

Whether we are competitors or recreational riders, each of us experiences this mixture of brilliant, acceptable and sub-standard performances. It seems that most riders are unable to explain these variations, but rationalize them as part of life's haphazard progression. However, while many people will accept such an explanation for their performances, it is not really the truth. If we think about it, there are many variable factors which can affect the quality of our rides, and most of these can be identified – which is the first step towards controlling and remedying them.

Obviously, there are some factors, such as personal health or circumstances, or physical problems with the horse, which it would be inappropriate for this book to address. There is, however, one major factor for consideration which is often overlooked, yet has a great influence upon the cycle of peaks, valleys and plateaux. This factor, which is referred to as progressive skill development, takes account of where we and our horses are in the process of acquiring new skills, and what stage we are at in our weekly, monthly or annual plans. Through studying this concept we can, at the very least, gain a better understanding of why we and our horses have previously performed, or are currently performing, at the levels achieved.

PROGRESSIVE SKILL DEVELOPMENT

Most commonly, variations in the quality of our performances can be attributed to the chronological stage we are at in acquiring, integrating and implementing our skills. Published work on expertise has asserted that skill progression follows at least a three-stage process. For our purpose as riders, there are times when we acquire new skills, times when we automate these new-found skills, and periods where we integrate them into our established riding styles. Let us see how these times relate to the theory of peaks, valleys and plateaux.

VALLEYS – A TIME OF SKILL ACQUISITION

Progressive learning is a fascinating experience that occurs in a cyclic fashion. Let us assume that we enter the cycle having at least a few riding skills that have served us well in the past. Each of these skills is integrated into a package – our unique riding style – which can be employed without a whole lot of thought. However, as we learn a new skill, what usually happens is that this alters at least part of our general skill applications. Riding skills which once seemed proficient and easy become awkward, deliberate, and mechanical. For varying amounts of time, depending on the complexity of the skill, there is an overall lowering of performance level. Although this temporary decrease in proficiency is understandable, we sometimes become frustrated, and lose patience with ourselves, our horses, or our trainers. The following case study highlights what can happen story during a skill acquisition phase.

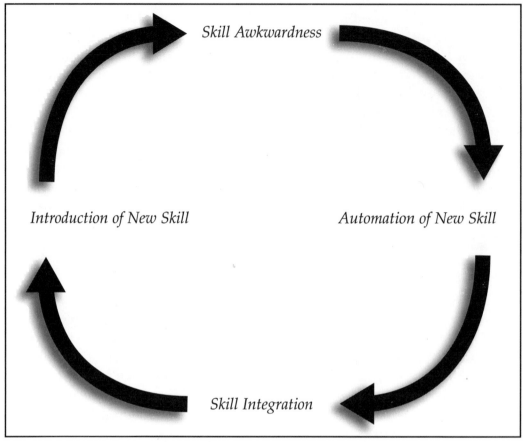

Figure 3: The Cycle of Skill Development

Case study

Miriam was an extremely gifted dressage rider. As well as creating an aesthetically pleasing picture on her horse, she almost always rode with sensitivity and feel. While she was participating in a month-long training clinic, she made some positive progress. During the first week of the clinic, the training consultant and rider focused on basic flat-work, with the trainer providing minor corrections to the horse–rider combination. At this stage, Miriam felt comfortable with the situation. Once the trainer and rider had established a positive relationship, the next logical step was to begin working on some more specific and detailed areas for progression. However, as trainer and rider began to explore what was new, uncharted territory for the rider, some resistances to the learning process began to emerge. Miriam began to feel that her riding was becoming awkward, deliberate and 'unnatural'. Although her trainer attempted to explain that valleys were a natural part of skill development, Miriam began to feel a loss of control, and therefore challenged her trainer's assistance. As a result, she prolonged the valley phase of her skill development instead of expediting the learning process.

If we apply common sense, we can appreciate that a new skill will become better and more comfortable with continued practice. However, more often than not, riders and other athletes seem to fight this part of the learning process. This is understandable, because no one ever wants to feel and appear clumsy, as opposed to proficient. Bodies and minds naturally stiffen when attempting to do something unfamiliar and awkward. When working with riders and athletes at this stage of their skill development, we help them in this matter by asking the following questions:

Is the skill being developed bringing you closer to your long-term goals?

How will developing this skill help you to meet long-term objectives? (This emphasizes the importance of integrating the new skill into the personal performance package.)

Is your current performance expectation realistic while a new skill is being acquired?

What would be a realistic performance expectation while the new skill is being acquired?

Together, we explore these interesting questions and, as a result, the client is reminded of the benefits derived from learning a new skill. Once we remember *why* we are learning a new lesson, we seem to become more forgiving of ourselves during times of difficulty. We are then able to re-establish a more positive overall perspective of our sport and our progress. Finally, by accepting the realities of our situation, we make the learning process easier.

PLATEAUX – A TIME OF SKILL INTEGRATION

After a period of deliberate practice, we eventually become comfortable with our recently acquired skill; we integrate the new technique or knowledge into our riding repertoire. Think back for a moment to the first time you were taught a riding skill that now seems effortless – like rising to the trot. Can you remember the circumstances, and some of the difficulties that you encountered? Like all beginners, you were asked to rise out of the saddle during one moment of the exercise, and then were more than happy to sit in it again. Just as you were about to relax, your instructor said 'rise' once more. After hearing 'up-down, up-down, up-down' for a few consecutive lessons, you were able to perform the action on your own. Reflecting on the initial awkwardness, you probably recall receiving a few extra bumps as you rose on the wrong diagonal. Eventually, you learned to rise comfortably on the correct diagonal so that you were in harmony with the horse's movement. The point is, we all undergo learning patterns similar to this throughout our riding careers – and we also progress at different speeds. Here are some suggestions on how to ease and speed up your own learning in the future:

- Become familiar with the mechanical principles and details associated with the skill.
- Accept that, at first, your practice will feel awkward and forced.
- Allocate time during each ride to practise your new skill, because continuity is important.
- Whenever possible, early practice of a new skill should be done at slower gaits or speeds, with plenty of thinking time between attempts. Increase the speed and complexity of the exercise step by step once you are comfortable with your current response to the challenge.
- Try to remain patient and do not attempt to force your personal progress.

Regardless of what new skill you are attempting to learn, as you seek to absorb it, your first aim will be to develop a sense of proficiency and ease. During the plateau, you will probably apply the newly developed skill and its mechanics in much the same way as was taught you by your trainer. However, your learning process will not end at this stage. You will realize, consciously or subconsciously, that you have your own, unique way of applying the new skill – an approach which is compatible with your own personal riding philosophy and style. Although you may not intentionally adapt each skill to suit your own style of riding, this is what will happen, and it will lead eventually to a new peak performance.

PEAKS – A TIME FOR FLOW PERFORMANCE

Precisely what constitutes a peak performance will vary with the individual, since peak performances are experienced by recreational riders, novices and international competitors alike. However, an international show jumper, for example, may have experienced a first peak or 'flow' performance as a child in the pony division and, undoubtedly, this experience will be compatible with the eventual peak performance in a Grand Prix. Furthermore, regardless of our riding disciplines or contexts, there are certain common denominators that we share when riding at our peak. These components include: the use of intuition; confidence and trust in ourselves and our mounts; the ability to be completely absorbed in the moment. When these components occur all together for the dressage partnership, horse and rider can appear as a single unit in flowing motion – much like a centaur.

Task 24. As you doubtless know, a centaur is a mythical figure, half man and half horse. During our rides, we aspire to become one with our horses. Only then do we truly experience peak performance. Below is a guided meditation for dressage and flat-work. Its emphasis is on melding you and your horse into one. We recommend that riders employ this exercise when they are undergoing difficulties in their partnership whilst on the flat.

Find a comfortable chair to sit in where your back is straight yet relaxed, your legs are slightly apart and your feet are touching the floor. Let your arms rest quietly by your sides, and place your hands on your lap in front of you. Close your eyes, take a deep breath and allow your diaphragm to fill. Hold the breath for five seconds, exhale and relax, and repeat this process five times. With each progressive breath, feel yourself moving more deeply into a state of relaxation. Appreciate the feeling of complete muscle relaxation.

Next, allow your mind to draw you to your favourite riding place. Notice the sight, sound and scent of where you are. Look around and take it in: this is your place. You have nowhere else to go, and nothing else to do. This is your time to enjoy being where you are. Take another deep breath and allow your mind to relax totally.

Notice your horse being led to you, coat gleaming, ears pricked, anticipating your ride together. Now, you are walking toward your horse and, when you reach him, you extend your arm to stroke his neck. Your horse, in turn, responds by turning and nuzzling you. Slowly, you tighten the girth, and lower the stirrups. When you are ready, you mount up. As you are mounting, breathe in; absorb the smell of your horse and your tack. Check the girth, adjust your reins and, when you are ready, ask your horse to walk on. As he begins to walk, notice his rhythm; the motion of his muscles and back. Feel your own back absorbing the motion; flowing with each footfall. Notice, as you do so, that your own back is relaxing and melding with that of your horse.

When you are ready, ask your horse to trot, and then to canter. You need only think of a transition – the horse seems to read your mind and moves in accord with your every thought. As you both begin to warm up, your muscles become more supple and riding motions become more fluid. Feel the flowing motion as you move through the different gaits. The horse is becoming a part of you. It is as though you are one, with your mind controlling his body. Enjoy this feeling of unity. There is no movement too difficult to perform. You need only imagine the feeling and it is there. Notice this sensation. Allow your body to absorb all the feelings of this moment. This is your ride in all its perfection. You need only to close your eyes, breathe deeply, and you can return to this special feeling whenever you wish.

When you are ready, slowly lift your chin and take a deep, relaxing breath. You begin to notice the sounds of the room where you are sitting. When you are ready, you may open your eyes. Do not stand up too quickly. Enjoy the feeling of peacefulness and restfulness. When you are ready, stand up, and stretch.

A rider interested in show jumping or cross-country will require a different form of guided meditation from that above. Instead of imagining horse and rider as one inseparable unit, this time they are regarded as two entities in complete harmony. The role of the rider is to follow the horse's every movement. The horse, in turn, has complete freedom to soar effortlessly over fences as if he were Pegasus.

Task 25. This second meditation will focus on the flow experience over fences. It is helpful when you wish to improve your horse – rider harmony over fences. Note that the first few sentences are

similar to those found in Task 24. However, once you mount your horse, the guided meditation will emphasize the soaring motion of jumping. We have purposely avoided deliberate description so that each individual can form their own mental picture of the riding area and type of fence.

Find a comfortable chair to sit in where your back is straight yet relaxed, your legs are slightly apart, and your feet are touching the floor. Let your arms rest quietly by your sides and place your hands on your lap in front of you. Close your eyes, take a deep breath and allow your diaphragm to fill. Hold the breath for five seconds, exhale and relax, and repeat this process five times. With each progressive breath, feel yourself moving more deeply into a state of relaxation. Appreciate the feeling of complete muscle relaxation.

Next, allow your mind to draw you to your favourite riding place. Notice the sight, sound, and scent of where you are. Look around and take it in; this is your place. You have nowhere else to go, and nothing else to do. This is your time to enjoy being where you are. Take another deep breath, and allow your mind to relax totally.

Notice your horse being led to you, coat gleaming, ears pricked, anticipating your ride together. Now, you are walking toward your horse and, when you reach him, you extend your arm to stroke his neck. Your horse, in turn, responds by nuzzling you in reply. Slowly, you tighten your girth, and pull your stirrups down. Then, when you are ready, you mount up. As you are mounting, you breathe in; absorb the smell of your horse and your tack.

While you are walking in your riding arena, appreciating the perfect going, you notice that a friend on the ground has thoughtfully set up two inviting fences: a small vertical on one side and a small oxer on the other. Both fences are of perfect height and width for you and your horse. When you are ready, ask your horse to trot on. Notice how attuned and receptive he is to your commands. Now, ask your horse to move into canter. As he responds, you both move forward easily in a slow, rhythmic gait. As you canter, you notice the energy and power in the horse's hindquarters; you and your horse have established a relaxed, yet energetic rhythm. Checking your horse's attentiveness, you ask him to extend, and then return to a more collected canter. The horse responds willingly to every signal and remains light in your hands as you both move effortlessly around the arena. Feeling comfortable and ready, you approach the first fence – the vertical. The horse's ears are pricked in delight as he approaches the obstacle rhythmically. You see a great stride and, as you reach the take-off point, you soften the contact. In response, the horse clears the fence with ease. Then, you circle and approach the fence again. Once more, the horse responds, demonstrating his willingness and agility. Now, it is time to jump the oxer. On the approach, you feel the compressed energy of the horse. Meeting the fence perfectly, you release this energy, and the horse soars effortlessly upward. You can feel his power as he lengthens and elevates his body in answer to your aids. You feel as if your horse has become Pegasus – a mythical winged creature.

In answer to your unspoken wish, you notice that your friend on the ground has raised the oxer. Full of confidence, you turn and approach the fence a second time. As if in slow motion, the horse gathers himself together, and you release him automatically. He pushes off from his hindquarters and stretches upward, toward the sky. You are airborne, and it feels an eternity before you softly touch down.

After this jumping warm-up, you know that you and your horse can meet any challenge. Together you are a formidable pair. Calmly, you bring your horse back to walk, and pat him. Both of you stretch and luxuriate in a job well done. Allow your body to absorb all the feelings of this moment. This is your ride in all its perfection. You need only to close your eyes, breathe deeply, and you can return to this special feeling whenever you wish.

When you are ready, slowly lift your chin and take a deep, relaxing breath. You begin to notice the sounds of the room where you are sitting. When you feel ready, you may open your eyes and begin to look around. Do not stand up too quickly. Enjoy the feeling of peace and restfulness. When you are ready, stand up, and stretch.

The guided meditations in Tasks 24 and 25 help to facilitate peak performances. If you can 'see' and 'feel' yourself and your horse performing to the highest of standards, then these are what you will aspire to. Beyond acting as goal-setting tools, the guided meditations will also help put you in touch with what it might be like to experience a peak performance with your mount. Together, a positive goal and a kinesthetic sense of the perfect ride will enhance your chances of achievement. You can also increase your chance of experiencing 'flow' through seasonal planning. We always say that if you really want to achieve a peak performance, you must plan for it systematically within a time frame. Let us now examine why this is so.

PERFORMANCE CYCLES DURING EACH YEAR

For the competitor, flow experience – or the lack of it – is also a consequence of seasonal planning. The reason for this is simple: out of the competition season, most of us devote much time to the development and refinement of skills. However, while we are engaged in skill revision, we tend to lose our competitive sharpness. Re-establishing competition polish takes time, and this must be taken into account when competition schedules are mapped out.

Flow experience – or the lack of it – is also a consequence of seasonal planning.

Depending on which discipline we compete in, and also where we reside, our competition season segments will vary. Many competitors plan their seasons chronologically, expecting that certain peaks, valleys, and plateaux will occur at specific times. For a top European three-day event rider, peaks would no doubt be planned for Badminton in the spring, and an international competition such as Boekelo or Burghley in the autumn. Valleys are opportunities to recharge personal energy levels and hone new skills, so these processes will be planned to occur during the off-season. Plateaux also have their place in the yearly cycle, ideally early in the season, when competition skills are being automated or re-established. Thus, regardless of which discipline you are involved in, there is a lead-up and let-down to each season. The proper planning of these segments assists optimal preparation, and thereby enhances the chance of peak performances.

Recreational riders can also develop a yearly riding plan aimed at achieving objectives. These objectives might include taking a riding holiday, or signing on for a clinic. Such recreational objectives can be planned and prepared for, with progress being made toward the ulti-mate objective. Springtime goals might include polishing up old skills and acquiring new ones – or even re-familiarizing yourself with the wide open spaces after a cold and snowy winter with nothing but indoor riding. In all such cases, what is effectively an off-season period can be employed to refine necessary skills. In the lead-up period to your main objective – your 'early season' – these new skills can be employed in a suitable riding environment. Then, once you are confident and well prepared, you will be able to succeed in achieving a peak performance in your main objective.

Task 26. The vast majority of athletes develop formalized seasonal plans. When doing so, they usually begin by selecting a few key competitions or objectives for the year. They then identify a progression of preparatory competitions and the acquisition of new skills, which will lead them towards their main goals. Consider the following questions, and incorporate what you learn from your responses into next season's performance plan.

1. Do you establish clear performance objectives from the start of the season onward? If so, do you include the acquisition of physical skills and feelings of proficiency as well as competition results?
2. Do you deliberately monitor the progression of your skills and your mental attitude in the lead-up to every performance, as well as to your 'key' tests?
3. If your answer to the previous question is 'yes', do you employ the information gained to learn key lessons, and to monitor your progress toward your main objectives?

SUMMARIZING PEAKS, VALLEYS AND PLATEAUX

In this chapter we have provided some explanations as to why riders experience peaks, valleys, and plateaux. There is a tendency to ascribe variations in performance to coincidence, and some superstitious people attribute their performances to luck. However, there are many perfectly logical explanations for these differences in performance. In the first place, it is helpful for each of us to gain a personal awareness of how we learn, at what stage of the season we learn best, and the amount of time we need to allocate for the integration of new skills. We should also understand that a feeling of awkwardness is normal when we enter uncharted territory. Accepting this and preparing for it will allow us to pass through this phase quickly. Some of us may fear making mistakes, yet one cannot learn without trial and error, and improvement comes through repetition.

If we remember that there are distinct stages in learning, and that the process engenders feelings which are common to us all, then we can learn more quickly and easily. We must become accustomed to the idea that, in the learning process, there is progression from awkwardness to proficiency, and we must plan around this phase of skill acquisition. There is an old saying: 'When we fail to plan, we plan to fail.' As riders, we must plan and prepare in order to achieve our aims. In short, when we take the initiative, we cease to be victims of circumstance.

REMINDERS ON PEAKS, VALLEYS, AND PLATEAUX

- Remember that there is a natural cycle of learning; appreciate the positive qualities that each segment of the cycle offers.
- Be aware of your own step-by-step progress within the learning cycle.
- Plan for your peaks, valleys and plateaux to occur at appropriate times in your training schedule.

FURTHER READING

Chamberlin, C., and Lee, T. 'Arranging practice conditions and designing instruction', in R. N. Singer, M. Murphey, and L. K. Tennant (eds.), *Handbook of research on sport psychology*, (New York, Macmillan 1993), pp.213-41.

Dodds, P. ' Cognitive and behavioral components of expertise in teaching physical education, *Quest*, vol. 2, (1994), pp.153-166.

Ericsson, K. A., Krampe, R. T., and Tesch-Rmer, C. ' The role of deliberate practice in the acquisition of expert performance',

Psychological Review, vol. 3, (1993), pp.363-406.

Goc-Karp, G., and Zakrajsek, D. B. ' Planning for learning - Theory into practice?', *Journal of Teaching in Physical Education*, vol. 6, (1987), pp. 377-92.

Thomas, J. T., Thomas, K. T., and Gallagher, J. D. 'Developmental considerations in skill acquisition', in R. N. Singer, M. Murphey, and L. K. Tennant (eds.), *Handbook of research on sport psychology*, (New York, Macmillan 1993), pp.73-105.

CHAPTER 7
THE COMPETITION-
EXHIBITION PACKAGE

Learn to add all new dimensions
to your present and future...
in belief of who you are
reach for the highest accomplishment
touch it, grasp it...
Diane Westlake

Many have wondered why some succeed while others experience difficulty in the heat of competition. Some people have inordinate amounts of talent, yet have problems reproducing their riding skills on the day of the competition. Others, when placed under pressure, somehow manage to perform beyond everyone's expectations. There is one distinct difference between these two groups of people. Those who are successful at the highest level seem to have consolidated their competition procedures, whereas others tend to vary their competition tactics with each performance, never identifying and refining techniques with which they feel comfortable. In this chapter, we will discuss how to put together a package that will help you realise your potential under competition conditions. Some of the recommendations will relate to principles discussed previously. Other concepts will be addressed for the first time. All, however, will be tailored specifically to the theme of enhancing your show and competition performance.

COMPONENTS OF THE COMPETITOR'S PACKAGE

There are various components to be considered in the competitive package. Each makes a contribution to our eventual competition results. In 1996, we helped to prepare competitors from five national teams for the Olympic and Para-Olympic Games. Some athletes had previously adhered to formalized competition procedures, and others had not. However, by the end of the two-day workshops, all of them had developed or refined the following components: competition simulations, packing, travelling, arrival on-site, training on-site, showground familiarization, eating, sleeping and competition procedures. Many of the strategies involved can be employed by you, regardless of your performance level, to achieve optimal results.

You will find that the competition package we are about to discuss will follow a chronological format, starting with the general pre-competition preparation of skills, and culminating with the completion of your first show. At the end of each show, this cycle will begin again, continuing until the season is completed.

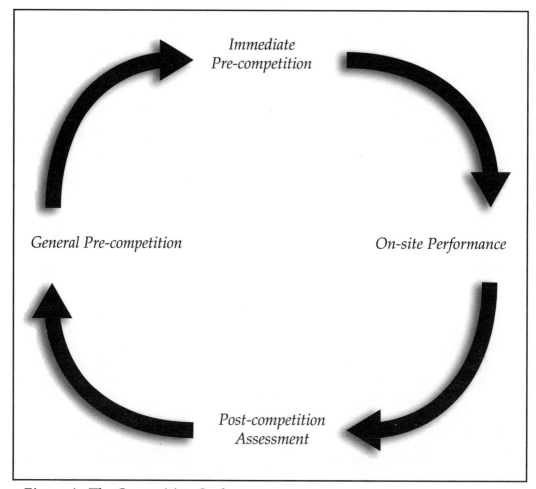

Figure 4: The Competition Cycle

TIME MANAGEMENT AND ORGANIZATION

The journey toward the competition season begins well in advance of the first show. A pro-active competitor is one who sets goals and then takes personal responsibility for seeing them through. Although the competition season may be of relatively short duration, the job of being a competitor is a year-round process. During the off-season, many of us seize the opportunity to regroup; to look after ourselves, our equipment, and our horses. You may find stationery stores selling 'Year At A Glance' calenders. These are simply large posters with the whole annual calendar displayed. Although some people may dislike their appearance, these calendars are very handy for establishing competition schedules and off-season and pre-season maintenance plans.

Task 27. Purchase this year's calendar poster. Fill in your competition dates, and also pencil in dates where you will schedule the following components:
- **Personal time management – significant non-equestrian affairs**
- **Maintenance and tack repair**
- **Wardrobe update and repair**
- **Trailer and lorry maintenance**
- **Personal health tasks, including your dental and physical checkups**
- **Horse's health tasks, including physical check-ups, inoculation and worming**
- **A progressive riding schedule**
- **Fitness programmes for you and your horse**
- **Nutrition evaluation for off-season and competition season, for horse and rider**
- **Renewal of your riding association memberships.**

PRE-COMPETITION SIMULATIONS

Once you and your horse have acquired the necessary levels of ability and fitness, there are further methods of preparing for forthcoming events. Simulations (dress rehearsals) are dry runs where you can replicate show conditions. When developing simulations, there are certain common guidelines to follow, regardless of the discipline involved. These progress as follows:

1. Understand the principles behind the required riding skills, and develop the ability to execute them.

2. Practise the required skills individually before attempting them as a complete test.

3. Once each component skill is mastered, practise combining two or three skills in a mini routine.

4. Simulate the whole routine in an ideal training environment.

5. Start to incorporate single distractions, including difficult ground conditions, poor weather, and a noisy environment.

Start to incorporate distractions, including difficult ground conditions, poor weather and a noisy environment.

6. Practise your routine whilst incorporating several distractions concurrently.

7. If possible, carry out your simulation at an unfamiliar training ground.

Below are simulation strategies for dressage, show jumping and riding cross-country. Each adheres to the progression described above.

Dressage simulation

We recommend the following methodical procedure. Start by looking over your test and becoming familiar with its movements, and their sequence. Then draw one scale diagram of the dressage arena for each movement, being as precise as possible with each diagram. Mark out each movement in sequence on the appropriate diagram: we suggest that you mark all walk work with dots, trot work with dashes and canter work with a solid line.

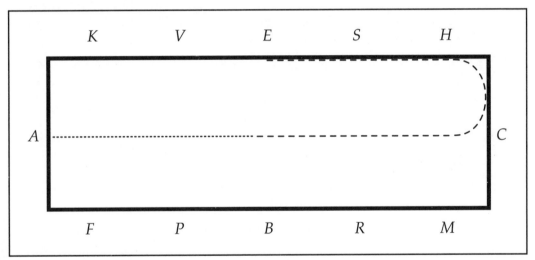

Figure 5: 60 x 20 m Dressage Arena to Scale

Once you have the intricacies of the dressage test memorized, it is time to start your physical preparation by riding individual components of the test. Once you feel comfortable with these, combine the components first into individual movements, then into segments consisting of four or five movements. Depending on the level of difficulty, the test can be partitioned into between three and six segments. Practise these, and refine each one until you happy with the results. Then, practise larger sections of the test by combining the segments until you are able to produce a complete, polished dressage routine.

In the week before the test, ride simulations from warm-up onward in breeches, hat, gloves and jacket, on a plaited horse. The objective here is to become re-acquainted with your show clothing and warm-up procedure. Riders competing at the higher levels should also consider including mock judges at C and the quarter-lines, or at B and E. You might also consider having noisy people with umbrellas and dogs near the dressage arena, so that you can develop or refine your strategies for coping with distractions before departing for your competition.

Show jumping simulation

Start by jumping a small vertical and then an oxer in the middle of a warm-up arena. Once you feel comfortable jumping individual fences of the required dimensions, practise segments of two and three fences, first with straight lines and conventional distances, and then with curving approaches and more difficult striding. Next, include an appropriate variety of more difficult fences in each segment. Once you feel comfortable with these, increase the number of fences until you have a complete course containing 12–15 jumping efforts. Once you have jumped this to your satisfaction, measure the whole course, and ride it at the speed specified in the forthcoming competition. Then, if the competition is pure show jumping, practise jump-off turns. In the week leading up to the competition, practise your full simulation with start and finish markers, 'ring officials', and any distractions that you or your horse need practice to cope with.

Cross-country simulation

Unlike those for dressage and show jumping, the cross-country simulation may have to begin by working at the required speed. Therefore, begin your simulation by galloping in a large field or on a track with a suitable surface. During your gallops, practise increasing and decreasing your speed, and altering the degree of impulsion as necessary for your level of competition. Ride in the correct posture, with the same length of leathers as you will be using in your competition.

Once you feel comfortable with all aspects of galloping, begin to tackle individual, straightforward obstacles. Then, practise riding short courses of 3–5 fences in succession. At this point, make sure that you feel happy with your performance. Next, practise larger segments, until you feel comfortable with a course of 10–12 fences. Although your competition courses will be longer than this, the intensity of the proposed practice course is adequate. Make sure that the obstacles over which you practise are of equivalent difficulty and dimension to those that you and your mount will encounter in the next competition. As a last step, ride in your competition equipment – and try including a tack check, start box, timer, and inclement weather in your simulation.

(Note that, if you are an event rider, you will have the arduous task of riding simulations from all three disciplines.)

Task 28. Now is the time to plan a simulation strategy that is suited to yourself, your horse and your competition discipline. As you work out the details, log your progress using the following criteria.

1. Have you memorized the intricacies of each dressage movement, or just the general route, tansitions and paces?

2. During physical preparation, are you beginning with single components before moving on to larger segments? Consider refinements to how you will prepare progressively for your next simulation.

3. Once you have practised the complete routine, which distractions or challenges do you want to include for the next time? Make a list and plan ahead.

4. Having completed your competition simulation, are there any distractions that you might want to include or exclude next time?

PREPARATION AND PACKING INVENTORIES

As the competition draws nearer, many of us embrace set procedures that help round off our preparation. These actions usually indicate that we are putting the finishing touches to our pre-competition strategies. Some riders go for a haircut, a massage, do some last-minute shopping, or have an evening out before departing to the competition. Others take time to themselves, rent a video, or review footage from previous competitions. When developing your own strategy, always remember that your plan should suit your temperament and experience. When dealing with concerns about performance, try to identify activities that restore a relaxed and positive perspective. Anything that promotes confidence and self-esteem will directly benefit your performance. Here are some suggestions: have a favourite, comforting meal; listen to relaxing music; take a long shower; spend time with undemanding people – and employ some of the relaxation exercises mentioned in previous chapters.

Packing procedures are very important in maintaining a positive frame of mind. Everyone has a conventional packing list, but we propose that your list should extend beyond riding equipment. As horse-lovers, we try to care for our horses as well as possible, but we often forget to care for ourselves. Depending on how you adjust to hotel rooms, caravans, or camping, you might want to consider packing your own pillow, favourite shower gel, shampoo, and other self-care products. You should also take some comfortable clothing for travelling, evenings out, and rest periods. In short, pack items that are necessary, familiar and calming.

FORMALIZED PROCEDURES ON-SITE

Arriving at the competition site tends to create uncertain feelings for many competitors. Your comfort level, however, can be increased by pre-planning each of the following: greeting other competitors, unpacking, familiarizing yourself with the show grounds, fulfilling on-site training, developing general eating and sleeping procedures, preparing to compete on the day of the competition, warming-up, and performing. All of these on-site procedures will now be discussed.

Greeting other competitors

The way in which you interact with other competitors and officials can have a major impact on how you feel throughout the duration of the competition. It is therefore wise to plan an inter-personal approach that you feel comfortable with. Depending upon your values and priorities, you might decide to allocate time for socializing with friends and acquaintances, or you might wish to keep to yourself. Whatever your basic aim, the procedure can be fine-tuned so that you are comfortable with your social conduct and, at the same time, focused on your riding tasks.

In addition to planning how you will greet competitors and officials, consider also how you intend to respond to their behaviour. For example, many of us are good friends with other competitors. For some of our friends, however, competition is stressful and this stress may test even the most good-natured. As some of our fellow competitors become nervous, they may unintentionally respond to friendly overtures in a sharp and biting way. Therefore, we suggest that you not take anyone else's adverse behaviour as a personal affront when experienced in a competition context. Instead, it is a better policy to accept peoples' nervous responses as part of the competition environment. Furthermore, as we become more willing to accept the behaviour of others, they in turn, will become more tolerant of ours!   Therefore, rather than allowing minor personal issues to distract you from the task in hand, plan to concentrate on achieving your own competition goals, and enjoy the pursuit of each one.

Unpacking and familiarization with the grounds

Part of our initial on-site organization includes unpacking our equipment and scouting out the showground. Most competitors start the process of settling in by setting up their equipment. If you walk through a stabling site, you will learn a lot about riders' organization and comfort levels. Some never truly unpack. Instead, they keep their

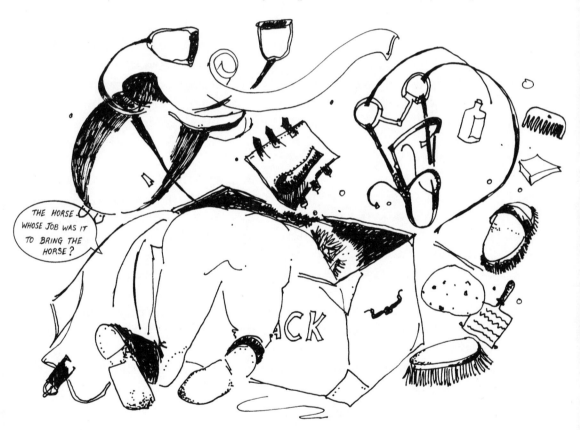

If you walk through a stabling site, you will learn a lot about riders' organization and comfort levels.

equipment locked away in trunks, and spend much of their time rifling through these to find the necessary item. Apart from being disorganized, such people never truly settle in to the show site. Indeed, through choosing not to unpack, they have psychologically planned a rapid retreat from the showground as soon as the competition has concluded. Other riders seem more organized: their rugs, bridle, saddle racks, feed and grooming kit are readily accessible. Because these people are well-organized both physically and mentally, they become more time-efficient and are necessarily more likely to perform to their expectations than disorganized performers.

Mental organization can be enhanced by familiarizing yourself with the showground. This process is important for several reasons: on the first level, you need to know where to find the show secretary, vet, farrier, ring steward, stable manager, and the individual competition arenas or courses. Once you know where everything is situated, you can begin the next step; planning your competition strategy. Using the information you have already gathered, you can establish where grooms need to be at given times, where you can train and warm-up your horses, and how long it will take you to reach the start box or competition arena from the practice ring. Furthermore, your knowledge of various show-ground features can be included in your competition imagery.

Competition imagery

This is a fundamental part of mental preparation for competition. Dressage and eventing riders will know what their arenas or cross-country courses look like at least one day before competing. We recommend that these riders image their performances a day or more before the competition from a rider's eye point of view, and include landmarks, ground and probable weather conditions, and an audience in the exercise.

Task 29. At your next competition or show, familiarize yourself with the showground. Then, either the day before or the day of your performance, image it as completely and accurately as possible. Focus on producing a perfect performance in the environment of your forth-coming competition.

TRAINING ON THE COMPETITION GROUND

At times, we have witnessed riders whose competition results have been adversely affected during on-site training sessions. A typical scenario would start with a nervous and spooky horse, to whom the rider responded with anger and impatience. After what would prove to be a long, arduous schooling session, the horse would finally give in to the rider's demands, but out of fatigue rather than willingness. During the next day's performance, the horse would typically be 'flat' – obedient yet unenthusiastic. Often, such difficulties are more the result of the rider's self-doubt and nervousness than anything else. To counteract these negative influences, we encourage all athletes and riders to see the competition as a 'leap of faith'. Realistically, by the time we arrive at the competition site, we have prepared to the best of our abilities. Now, it is time to let go and trust ourselves and our partners.

There is, however, a final training procedure that is both practical and constructive. We suggest that you commit yourself to an on-site training plan which, in addition to setting the tone for your forthcoming competition, also helps you and your horse become familiar with the sights and sounds of the showground. Whilst walking at the beginning of each session, use this time to show your horse all the parts of the showground that may be relevant to your forthcoming performance. Together, explore all pertinent areas until you both feel comfortable with the environment. Then, practise part of your warm-up routine on the flat as you will be doing it before the competition. Once you begin schooling, remember to keep the tone of the warm-up enjoyable so that you and your horse carry over a positive attitude into the next day. When you have completed your training session, reward yourself and your horse for a job well done by going for a peaceful walk around the showground. This relaxing and enjoyable ride will set the tone for next day's brilliant and fluid performance.

MENTAL PREPARATION THE NIGHT BEFORE COMPETING

The night before competing, each and every one of us likes to employ familiar routines and preparation strategies. As a start, allot yourself time for a relaxing shower or bath. Don't be afraid to pull out your favourite shower gel, shampoo, and other comforts. Once you have showered and changed, dine with chosen friends and supporters. If your support team consists of a groom, family members or close friends, these are the people you can turn to for encouragement. On the basis of your personal preference, you can either eat in a restaurant or cook your own food. Each of us has different comfort foods that seem to facilitate optimal performance, and eating these will help maintain a positive perspective. Try to develop a list of suitable favourite foods which are easily accessible at all competitions. Also, remember that the night before the competition is a prime opportunity to develop a positive attitude – so start to enjoy your show experience!

Once dinner is over, return to your sleeping quarters, and take some private time to prepare mentally for the forthcoming competition. Some riders like to image the night before a competition. If you wish to do so, there are several imageries you can choose from. Riding-related imagery would be preferable if you are an eventer who wants to review the cross-country course, gain familiarity with it, and enhance confidence. If you are a dressage rider, you might adopt a similar approach to a forthcoming test, or perhaps recall your best-ever performance of that test. Alternatively, if you are confident in your ability but still feel a little tense before your forthcoming performance, try a more relaxing imagery like the mental retreat discussed in Chapter 2.

Whatever mental strategy you select for yourself, be sure that it induces a positive attitude, clear thinking, and a sense of relaxation. All too often, people tend to select strategies that make them more nervous and therefore less focused.

If you tend to be a little anxious the night before competing, relaxation strategies might be the preferred form of mental preparation. Some of the possibilities include listening to soft music in a dimly lit room, practising deep abdominal breathing, employing progressive muscle relaxation, or even going for a quiet walk (relaxation techniques have been discussed in detail in Chapter 5). In this current chapter, we are emphasizing the importance of procedures that will comfort you and keep your mind and body relaxed. Inevitably, if you feel mentally and physically prepared for the next day's competition, it will be easier to settle down for a good night's rest.

GETTING A GOOD NIGHT'S REST

Many athletes and riders have experienced at least occasional difficulty in sleeping the night before a competition. If you are one of these people, there are a couple of ideas that you can try. First, any mental preparation should exclude performance-related imagery. Instead, we suggest that you practise one of the previously discussed guided meditations to soft, instrumental music which incorporates natural sounds. An alternative approach is to accept that you have prepared to the best of your ability and, rather than practising a specific mental strategy, go out and do something enjoyable.

Despite following these suggestions, it is a fact that people sometimes remain restless the night before competing. If this ever happens to you, do not get frustrated with yourself. People can function at their best on less than optimal amounts of sleep provided that they are well rested. Therefore, allow your body to relax by accepting that you are experiencing a sleepless night. By doing so, you will conserve energy that would otherwise have been expended in frustration and anger.

COMPETITION DAY STRATEGIES.

The competition should always be a positive time. Competing is an opportunity to measure your training and preparation strategies against others. Perhaps your approach will be successful; perhaps it will require revision. Either way, seen in its right perspective, competition will provide you with some helpful hints on how to perform under pressure. Moreover, if you are receptive to the experience, you can learn some useful lessons about yourself and your horse.

Start competition day by having a healthy, sustaining breakfast. Far too often, we have seen competitors pay special attention to their horses' diets and neglect their own. You require sufficient nourishment and plenty of fluids in order to perform at your best. Therefore, no matter what, make certain that you nourish yourself – even if you find it a difficult process. However, be sure to eat foods that will not upset your stomach or tax your digestive system.

Once you have eaten your breakfast, return to your preparation routine. This may vary from taking some quiet time to yourself to putting on your show clothing and preparing your horse and equipment for the day's events. Whatever activities you select, be sure that they help to focus your energies, rather than diffusing them.

Task 30. Identify some activities that would help prepare you for an imminent performance. Note each one and, before your next competition, let your support team know that you would like to do these things for yourself.

Soon after you have finished preparing yourself and your equipment, your time to perform will arrive. When it is time to warm-up, put your pre-determined programme into action. As you settle in to it, be sure to follow the same procedures that you did during training. Adhering to a concrete warm-up strategy will engender a sense of comfort and familiarity for both you and your horse. Make sure that each component of the warm-up is given due attention, and that none is overlooked or rushed. Enjoy each moment – you worked hard to get there.

During this time, your trainer should also have a pre-determined role. Some riders will prefer active coaching, others will prefer their trainer to intervene only when necessary. (If you have not developed a warm-up routine until now, start experimenting under the guidance of an expert trainer. Before long, you will be able to establish the warm-up procedure that works best for you and your horse.)

Task 31. Write down a competition warm-up strategy that is suitable for you and your horse. In doing so, identify the components of the warm-up, their basic sequence, and how much time you will allot to the following:
Walk work
Trot work
Canter work
General warm-up (transitions or simple fences)
Tune-up (more difficult movements or fences)
Last-minute information from your trainer.

STRATEGIES IN THE ARENA

Once the time comes to enter the competition arena, your preparation is completed. All that remains is to allow yourself and your horse to do what comes naturally. There are, however, a few minor strategies that can be called upon to enhance your performance. If you are a dressage rider, try to display a little showmanship and, no matter what, portray a picture of confidence. By doing so, you will feel stronger and more self-assured. Regardless of the competition discipline, you will also have some sort of performance strategy to follow. For instance, the show jumper might divide the course into four sections. Then, specific parts of the jumping strategy can be employed in each one. In the first part, which includes the start line and the first two fences, the rider can plan to develop a forward, relaxed rhythm, and get accurate strides to each fence. During the second part – the main portion of the course – the rider can plan to add impulsion, or to maintain rhythm and flow. Often, in the third section – the third- and second-to-last fences – riders might remind themselves and their horses to remain focused and accurate. Then, in the final section – the last fence and the finish line – riders usually concentrate on a heightened awareness, sustained accuracy, a burst of speed and power to the finish line, and a quiet easing down. (Although this is a show jumping example, dressage and cross-country riders can develop similar competition plans.)

Task 32. Divide your dressage, cross-country or show jumping test into four parts (the start and the first few movements/obstacles, the

body, the last few movements/obstacles, and the finish). Develop strategies for each of these four segments, and pre-plan them into your performance. Then, after you have completed your competition, assess the result with reference to your performance in each segment.

POST-COMPETITION FEELINGS

Before we discuss in detail the value of analysing your performance, we should acknowledge the sometimes disquieting emotional response that may follow immediately in the wake of a major performance. The scenario, by no means uncommon, is as follows.

You have prepared for weeks – maybe months. Some top competitors may have prepared for years. You have developed a partnership with your horse; worked with your trainer; kept a journal; prepared yourself mentally. Indeed, you have done all you can do in your preparation for 'the big one'. Whether this is an inter-club competition, your first official horse trial, or an international championship, this is it.

You've done it. You've done really well – you may even have won it. Congratulations! So why are you feeling so empty inside? This happens to many people. Olympic athletes, after winning a medal, have been known to ask: 'Is this all?'

If you have planned for weeks or months, it may take anything from a few hours to a few days to wind down. If you have prepared for years, it may take several months before the internal dust settles. The bigger the stakes and the longer the preparation time, the longer it will take you to get back to being yourself.

This is something that most people do not prepare or plan for, when perhaps they ought to. When planning your competition season, you might begin a post-show tradition, such as a dinner where you can simply relax, down-load your feelings and share a quiet celebration with those close to you. You might even ask that they listen to your performance assessment without criticizing you at this time. Later, when you are ready, you will ask for their opinions and advice, but immediately after the competition it is important to be allowed to decompress. Similarly, your own final analysis, and the writing of your performance journal, should be left until you have given yourself a little time and gained some clarity of thought.

It is important to understand that the feelings described are to be expected, because planning for them and dealing with them will remove their sting and help you to move on more quickly towards your next goal.

POST-COMPETITION EVALUATION AND PERFORMANCE JOURNALS

Once you have completed the competition, it is time to assess your results. We would venture to say that the immediate post-competition period is the best time to refine your competition strategy. With each passing competition, we can learn many lessons about what works and what does not. Interestingly though, many competitors – even at the highest level – do not take the time to identify and evaluate these lessons. Do not fall into this error; once you have completed each competition, take some time to review your performance and learn from it.

After this, the next logical step is to log the lessons learned in a performance journal. This is necessary if you are going to take full advantage of the opportunity to assess your training and competition methods, note those which proved successful and revise others as appropriate. The reason for this is that, while the need to change some things will be immediately apparent to you, other factors may emerge only upon reflection, or once post-competition training begins. Therefore, when writing in your journal, be sure to include every aspect of training and competition performance including physical and mental preparation, mood, focus, activation, training and equipment used.

Task 33. Commit yourself to maintaining a performance journal. Start by purchasing a notebook, and logging all your results – both good and bad. Evaluate your performance in the following areas: your simulations, packing procedures, arrival on-site, training, diet, rest, mental preparation, and competition results.

SUMMARIZING COMPETITION PLANNING

When preparing for competition, most athletes concentrate on improving technical skill. Some, however, acknowledge the value of mental preparation, and a few will have deliberately incorporated a complete mental preparation package into their training and competition routines. A formalized plan of this type complements the development of physical skills, and we believe this represents the balanced approach to improving performance.

If you have never implemented mental strategies as part of your organized competition programme, you may be daunted by the thought of extra demands on your time. However, a part of the mental training programme includes time management and organization. Furthermore, many of the strategies discussed can be employed whenever you find yourself in a situation that entails waiting for something. Whilst in a dentist's waiting room, for example, you can write up your journal, practise your relaxation imagery, work on your deep breathing, refine your progressive muscle relaxation, or recollect your last peak performance. There are many such moments in each day, when you might be delayed by heavy traffic or late appointments. At such times, you might have experienced frustration, rage, and tension. However, you do not have to view these delays as wasting time – at such moments you can seize the opportunity to practise the skills that will enhance your competition performance and mobilize them for personal use. After a while, having turned such delays into valuable moments for yourself, you will become proficient in employing each strategy. Moreover, you will have taken a stressful situation and turned it to your own advantage, and taught yourself to move from a tension-filled personal environment to a calmer, more organized state. These are the very things you wish to do in competition, and thus you have practised exactly what you needed to practise.

REMINDERS FOR COMPETITION PLANNING

- Your competition plan begins long before the competition itself.
- By developing and refining your competition procedure, you will be a better organized and more confident performer.
- Share your competition procedures with your support team (your trainer, family, friends, and groom).
- Performance journals are the most accurate way of learning what serves you well in competition, as opposed to what does not.

FURTHER READING

Orlick, T. 'Implementing the plans', *Psyching for sport*, (Champaign, Illinois, Human Kinetics 1986), pp.71-8.

Orlick, T., and Partington, J., *Psyched - inner views of winning*, (Ottawa, Coaching Association of Canada 1986).

Rushall, B., 'Elite athletes at competition', *Psyching in sport: the psychological preparation for serious competition in sport'* (London, Pelham 1979), pp.17-23.

Savoie, J. 'It's showtime', *That winning feeling: A new approach to riding using psychocybernetics*, (North Pomfret, Vermont, Trafalgar Square 1992 [UK edn. London, J.A. Allen 1992]), pp.127-32.

Schinke, R. J. 'Putting together your competition package', *Australian Horse & Rider*, vol. 10, (1995), pp. 28-30.

CHAPTER 8
THE BALANCED PERSPECTIVE

What lies behind us and what lies before us
are tiny matters compared to what lies within us.
Ralph Waldo Emerson

Up to now, we have discussed specific sport psychology skills. However, strategies to enhance performance can broaden in scope to an area that we call 'the balanced perspective'. What do we mean by this? When we enter the equestrian world, we begin to experience its magic in many different contexts: appreciating the combined smell of hay, horses and tack; grooming and communicating with our horses; meeting other riding enthusiasts and sharing anecdotes; moments of harmony during lessons; riding in beautiful countryside. Such moments are just some examples of what is magical about our sport but really, every part is special in its own right. Sometimes, we tend to focus too much on one area, at the expense of our overall enjoyment. In truth, continued enjoyment lies in balancing each and every part of the equestrian experience. During this chapter, we will explore how to develop a balanced approach that will enhance both recreational and competitive riding, and also provide some suggestions on how to maintain it.

GROOMING TO MAINTAIN THE BALANCE

Grooming is a vital part of the horse – rider partnership. The act of grooming becomes a loving, caring touch between rider and horse, increasing the intimacy and trust which are so necessary at every level. It helps horse and rider bridge worlds. Therefore, grooming is one part of horsemastership that can facilitate a balanced perspective providing you see it in that light, rather than as a chore.

NOVICES AND THE ACT OF GROOMING
The act of grooming seems to settle both horse and rider, giving each a

chance to get to know the other. Riders new to the sport might, at first, feel somewhat intimidated by their proximity to the horse. Time spent in grooming allows them to become familiar with the size and shape of the horse, and with his unique temperament and personality. While the rider brushes the horse he, in turn, has the opportunity to sniff and nuzzle the rider, familiarizing himself through scent and touch. Grooming, then, becomes an initial step in forging an acquaintance which should bloom into a partnership.

Time spent grooming sets the tone for the ride to come. A rushed grooming, with little contact and care, may yield a less-than-satisfactory ride. The reason for this is simple: the more you give, the more you get. Thus a thorough, careful grooming should produce a relaxed horse and rider, ready to work in harmony. In the greater scheme of things this calm, unhurried approach will bear fruit for the future: comfortable rides and enjoyable experiences are preludes of sustained commitment to the sport.

ADVANCED RIDERS AND THE ACT OF GROOMING

Although they do not always do so, advanced riders should commit themselves to grooming their horses thoroughly. With such people, the horse – rider partnership is often well-established, yet complex. During training these partnerships experience moments of frustration as well as moments of harmony. Depending on the goals set, they may also spend more time working together than playing together. At this level, then, grooming takes on an added dimension: that of increasing mutual intimacy and trust. The extra time and care invested by the rider will benefit the partnership as a whole. Grooming is therefore a time for reconnecting and renewing the bonds of affection and trust. It is from such harmony that brilliance is produced.

TACKING-UP

After grooming, the act of tacking-up is a further step in the mental and physical preparation for your ride. Everyone ought to tack-up for them-selves – or at least check their tack thoroughly to ensure their own peace of mind. Just knowing that your tack and horse are clean and in good condition will put you at ease. Furthermore, careful, considerate tack-ing-up will reinforce your horse's trust in you.

THE BALANCED APPROACH TO RIDING

WARMING-UP

During this preliminary phase of the ride, horse and rider have the opportunity to prepare themselves mentally and physically, both as individuals and as partners. When ample time is allocated for this process, the partnership can approach the task ahead with supple bodies and clear, calm minds. If, on the other hand, the warm-up is hurried, it will prove less useful – perhaps even counter-productive. Remember, therefore, that learning and improvement are products of a carefully-constructed process, and that warming-up correctly is an integral part of a constructive ride.

THE RIDING AGENDA

Most riders plan their agenda well in advance of each ride; depending on the interest and goals of the individual, a routine is set. In order to maintain a balanced approach it is imperative to pre-plan structured lessons, opportunities to practise, and times to relax and play with your horse. Novice riders need to learn the fundamentals in a structured environment, but can also make use of hacking to integrate new skills and get much-needed riding mileage. Although advanced riders have different needs, these can be met through a basically similar regime. Since much of their time is spent in correcting and refining intricate techniques, the advanced combination benefits greatly from relaxing and playing together in a stress-free environment. By doing so, they become a complete partnership as opposed to having just a working relationship.

This brings us to an important point: riding should be fun – a shared adventure. Riders of all ages and levels benefit from riding outdoors, relaxing on their mounts, riding simply for the pure pleasure of it. Riding in the countryside does far more than just help the rider develop technical skills. It is a healing exercise, that soothes the raw nerves of the stressed business person, builds the confidence of the timid rider, and gives a foundation to the perspectives of the top performer. Riding in rhythm with Nature's sounds is immensely soothing to both horse and rider, and re-establishes a fresh and positive approach.

Task 34. If circumstances permit, consider the following when planning

your next ride in the countryside.

- Greet the dawn mounted, listening to the sounds of the forest or countryside as it awakens.
- Take a picnic lunch and go for an all-day ride with one or two of your closest friends.
- Try a ride at dusk. As the sun sets slowly through the trees, listen to the countryside quietening into the night.
- Have you ever ridden by the silvery light of a full moon?

Once you have completed one such ride, note how you felt about your sport during and immediately after the ride.

If we remember to bring a sense of playfulness to our riding...

At this point, let us share with you how we return to nature with our horses:

In our part of Canada, we have four distinct seasons. We believe that horses and riders alike enjoy the changes and benefits each has to offer. The sights, sounds, and scents of Nature change constantly and stimulate both our senses and those of our horses. All enjoy the warmth of the summer sun, the refreshing crispness of autumn, playing in the snow, and the fresh scent of new spring grass. Each one of these seasons has its respective advantages. For instance, in winter, when the snow is deep, it is good to get out of the arena, smell the cool scent of pines and listen to the snow crunching beneath under our horses' hooves. We can complain about the weather, or we can use the snow as an opportunity to 'leg-up' our horses. The horses enjoy hacking through the deep snow, and it is a great muscle developer as well as a spiritual adventure. When we play with our horses, we tend to their needs as well as our own. If we remember to bring a sense of playfulness to our riding, we and our horses will enjoy the schooling sessions for the challenges they present.

LIFE INFLUENCES RIDING

Sometimes, it can be difficult to bring a positive approach to a ride. Personal feelings can affect how we approach our sport, our horse, and our own abilities. Have you ever noticed that some days you approach your riding in a more postive way than others? Maybe this has something to do with other factors in your life. For example, when you visit the yard after a particularly difficult day at work, or after a quarrel with a loved one, you bring a certain heaviness to your ride. Your horse, being a very sensitive creature, is aware of your mood, and seems to mirror it in his performance. If, on the other hand, you have experienced a wonderful day with some of your best friends, the chances are that you enter the yard full of energy and prepared for a wonderful, enjoyable ride. At such times your horse, aware of your positive frame of mind, seems to make every effort to co-operate with you. In essence, then, the emotion that you bring with you into the saddle can influence the quality of ride that you experience. How we feel can affect how we ride – and also how we perceive our ride.

Thankfully, whatever the emotions we carry with us from our personal or professional lives, horses, riding, and the natural world can generally return us to a balanced state. We all have tough days. At times like these, we have two possible options: trying to immerse ourselves in a schooling session, or taking ourselves out into the countryside to relax. Whichever we choose, we must make sure that it will have a positive effect.

WINDING DOWN

The balanced approach to riding continues even as the ride comes to a close. Just as horse and rider moved gradually together during the grooming, tacking-up and riding phases, so they must gradually disengage as the ride comes to an end. Throughout the whole sequence of events, the temperaments of both horse and rider must be taken into account. We began the riding cycle by bridging worlds with our horses through the act of grooming and, having received the gift of a good ride, we must prepare to go our separate ways by winding down. Saying goodbye consists of unhurriedly removing the tack, doing whatever is necessary to make your horse comfortable and patting and playing with him. This sets the tone for your next ride – a time that you can both anticipate with pleasure.

Meditation for restoring the balance

The winding down process continues after you leave the yard. Upon returning home, you may wish to go one step further by relaxing into the forthcoming meditation of childhood reminiscences.

Dim the lights and disconnect the telephone so that there are no distractions. Loosen any tight clothing, relax in a chair, or lie down in a comfortable place. Ask someone with a pleasing voice to read the following exercise to you slowly and softly. At the same time, have some New Age or soft classical music playing in the background. You may also want to tape this exercise for continued personal use.

Take a few deep breaths, inhaling to the count of five, exhaling to the count of five. With each breath, feel yourself growing more and more relaxed. This is your time. There are no other demands on you. Simply close your eyes and, with each breath, feel your body move more deeply into a state of relaxation. There is nowhere you need to go and nothing that needs to be done. Enjoy the sensation of your body letting go of any tension it may be holding. Feel your jaw soften and your shoulders drop. Take another deep breath and let your diaphragm and stomach relax. Feel your legs relaxing and your hands and feet growing warmer. Enjoy the feeling of your totally relaxed, warm body.

magine that it is a warm summer's day and you are standing in a field of wild flowers. Smell their perfume, feel the warmth of the sun on your body, look all around you and take in Nature's beauty. As you scan the horizon, you see a child running towards you. Notice the child's grace and beauty. There is something familiar about this child. As the child draws closer, you realize that this child is you. As you reach down and lift this child in your arms, you seem to re-enter your childhood. You merge with the child and become one. You, the child, run through the field to a place where your pony is standing in the shade of a tree. Your heart is filled with joy. Your pony calls to you softly as you approach. You vault onto your pony's back and squeeze gently with your legs, urging your pony forward. You are experiencing a magical bareback ride; smooth and easy through fields of flowers. The daisies are so high that they tickle the bottoms of your bare feet. You and your pony are having another one of those special days that makes your childhood so great.

As you slow down to a walk, you notice that someone is calling. You approach. Drawing nearer, you dismount and lead your pony to that person. As you look up, it seems as though you have looked into the future and seen yourself as an adult. The adult reaches out to pick you up, and you welcome the embrace of strong arms and loving heart. The future looks good. Savour the moment and feel the strong yet totally relaxed body. Enjoy the moment.

When you feel ready, open your eyes slowly and allow yourself to adjust to the room you are in. This is your special place to return to whenever you need to relax.

MAINTAINING BALANCE DURING COMPETITION

In riding, the whole is greater than the sum of the parts. Throughout this book, we have emphasized the importance of the psychological, the emotional, the physical and the spiritual. Taken individually, each is only a small component. When we group all of these facets together, we increase our chances of reaching a balance with our sport and our individual rides.

A RETURN TO TIME MANAGEMENT

You might wonder why a balanced approach to the time we spend riding is so important. The reason is that many of us work under pressing time constraints. Haven't you ever felt torn between your desire to play and the obligation to work? With these conflicting feelings, it becomes difficult to bring a relaxed self to the sport. Should you wish to gain a better understanding of how you are balancing all aspects of your time, we invite you to examine the 'time pies' in Figure 6. Pie A can be sliced in proportion to the time you give weekly to friends, family, profession, community, personal relaxation, sport training, and any two additional categories that are also part of your life. This will give you a total of eight slices. Pie B can be your 'ideal time pie', representing how you would truly like to spend your spare time. You may find it interesting to compare how you actually spend your time with how you would truly wish to spend it.

Task 35. Take a few moments to complete time pies based on those in Figure 6. Then reflect on what you have learned about your time management. You may be pleased to find that you are managing your time beautifully. If you feel that you need to make changes, now is the opportunity to re-evaluate and revise your weekly agenda.

Pie A: My Present Time Pie   Pie B: My Ideal Time Pie

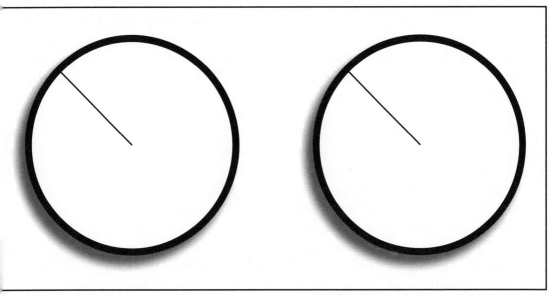

Figure 6: Time Pies

PARTNERSHIP IN FOCUS

Once you have completed organizing your time, it becomes easier to set and maintain your riding priorities. This, in turn, helps to keep the horse – rider partnership in focus. At times, you may experience another challenge. In your desire to progress, you may place more emphasis on your desired outcome than on the process. This is particularly apt to happen when preparing for a competition; the focus can shift from wanting a good ride to wanting a rosette. In such circumstances, horse and rider exhibit their tension in various ways. For instance, the horse's ears are no longer pricked; his tail swishes in dismay; he may wear a worried expression; the rider appears stiff and unforgiving. At such times enjoyment has left the ride and the partnership is in danger of losing its focus.

Case study

Recently, a young woman was having difficulty with her horse and, with each successive ride, she grew more frustrated. The horse, the other partner in this dilemma, was also experiencing his rider's impatience and refused to co-operate. The pair thus entered a downward spiral. Finally the rider, crying tears of rage, roared 'I can't ride any more'.

After a few minutes of calming discussion, the rider disclosed that she had wanted to win her competition so badly that she forgot her horse was her partner; she saw him as a vehicle for gaining glory. The horse, one can only assume, would not perform for a rosette, but would indeed perform for a thoughtful, caring partner. The pair are now happily working and playing together and improving their skills as a team.

WINDOWS OF OPPORTUNITY

Although riders can misplace their perspectives before and during competitions, they can also recapture them. Competitions offer unique 'windows of opportunity' for regaining or maintaining your positive perspective. Whenever a challenge is presented, we can be sure that there is a window of opportunity as well.

Task 36. During your next competition, it might be instructive for you to take the time to list as many windows of opportunity as you can find. To illustrate the idea, let us share with you one such experience.

Case study

We remember an important Young Riders and National Three-day event Team Selection Trial. It took place during the month of June, and the temperature was 32 degrees Celsius (90 degrees Fahrenheit), with 90 per cent humidity. We were all moving in slow motion. Some of the most advanced riders were lungeing their horses in the worst heat of the day; the early afternoon. The riders' faces were beet red, and their horses were wet, and moving sluggishly. As participants and observers, we thought that we might try something different.

There was no question that the horses needed to be exercised the day before this important competition. However, the heat was unbearable. What to do? On the property, a short walk from where we stood, was an inviting lake. We looked at it and made our decision. After asking permission from the estate's owner, we and the horses all went for a long, leisurely swim. As a result, the horses and riders had fun, cooled off, and were exercised – all at the same time.

Since the next few days were just as unbearable, we swam in the morning before each day's competition, and also in the evening after the events of the day were over. The results of this tactic were both illuminating and gratifying: when the final placings were announced, all three of our horses were in the top five of the Young Riders division, and made their respective teams. We did well and had a great time. Because we were able to re-focus, a balanced perspective was maintained. Being able to adapt, we were able to produce a positive outcome.

The challenge in this example was the heat. The window of opportunity that presented itself was the lake. Had there been no access to the lake, another option would have been available. In Canada, dusk falls at approximately 10 p.m., so the extended daylight hours would have allowed us to exercise the horses in the evening, when the heat of the day had abated.

When faced with a challenge, we should try to seek out as many options as possible. We cannot always adhere to a fixed schedule, but adaptability and flexibility will see us through difficulties. An adjustment to the realities of the situation, and an ability to find the best response, are what lead to a positive experience. We can bring our life skills to riding, and our riding skills to life. Competence coupled with flexibility improves any athletic performance. When we approach our challenges with self-assurance, we are able to see more clearly all the options available to us. Believing in ourselves strongly, we are able to seize the day.

Where some see confidence as a positive attribute, others might label it arrogance. If we allow ourselves to be vulnerable to such a critic, or if we seek approval from someone who is less than confident, then we allow ourselves to be disempowered. We must define ourselves positively and not allow tampering with that definition. When we allow others to define us, we are then risking the loss of our own true identity. In order to win we must feel positive, and take pride in our achievements. If we feel confident, really knowing in our hearts that we are good at what we do, then it becomes simple to go to a competition and do the job well. Being confident and taking pride in our achievements does not mean that we denigrate others, only that we enjoy our own skills.

THE WINNER'S CIRCLE

Every rider going to a competition would like to win. The reality is that there can only be one winner in each class of a horse show. Those who win consistently may begin to earn the envy of some of their fellow competitors. It may be a surprise to find out that others do not appreciate your win as much as you do. Also, winning a competition may stir up mixed feelings because some of the other competitors are friends of yours. When competing against friends, many athletes find it difficult to remain truly competitive. Indeed, some social psychologists believe that people perform better in a field of strangers than they do

When competing against friends, many athletes find it difficult to remain truly competitive.

in a field of friends. The question then becomes how to retain your friendships while still competing at your very best. There are several possible solutions to this dilemma. First, you might want to get together with some of your closest competition friends to share concerns. By doing so, you are all clearing the air with an open, honest discussion.

- Additional solutions employed by competitors in the past have included:
- Agreement to adopt an attitude of professionalism between competing friends for the duration of the show.
- Agreement that good sportsmanship is paramount.
- Agreement to socialize after, rather than during, the competition.

If you implement these suggestions, you are then empowered to perform fearlessly.

Task 37. Take a few moments to reflect on some of your past competition experiences, then list any times when you felt your performance suffered as a result of an outside influence. Next, reflect on each of the situations listed and provide a positive alternative that could improve your performance in a future competition.

A BALANCED TEAM APPROACH

Although horse shows are occasions when it may be prudent to maintain a little distance from our competition friends, we need not feel lonely. Competitions are the perfect opportunity to recognize and tap into the team support system that we have built.

Our support team will consist of many individuals: our vet and farrier, family members, trainer, grooms, friends and, perhaps, a sponsor. These peoples' belief in us re-affirms our belief in ourself. Our families are unwavering through good times and bad: they can be found every weekend driving the trailer to competitions, bringing along the picnic hamper and good cheer. Trainers, similarly, give of their time unstintingly. They have the combined role of providing emotional and technical support throughout the competition season. For those fortunate enough to have them, sponsors are an additional source of financial and emotional backing. Last – but definitely not least – grooms deserve special mention. Their task is to care for the horse and anticipate the rider's needs, and a good groom is an absolutely invaluable member of the team.

With a strong support team in place, we are better prepared for the show season. During the rigours of competition, we can become so immersed in our performance that we may forget to treat our supporters with the consideration they deserve. Simply remembering to say 'thank you' whenever appropriate will pay dividends for the future.

GIVING BACK

One thing that we can do for our sport when not competing is to volunteer our services to show organizers, local Pony Clubs and novice riders. Our sport is rich in the tradition of giving. Many have given to us and so we, too, should give to others. If we take, we must replace or we, in the end, become depleted. Thus giving back to our sport is another way of keeping the balance.

SUMMARIZING THE BALANCED PERSPECTIVE

In this chapter, we have looked at riding as being something more than the ride. Some of the components of a balanced approach are: the relationship between horse and rider; the blend of lessons and hacking in the countryside; establishing and maintaining equestrian friendships; the tradition of giving and taking and the ambiance of the sport. It is maintaining the balance between all parts of the equestrian experience that produces and then sustains riding enjoyment and excellence.

REMINDERS ON THE BALANCED PERSPECTIVE

- Remember to balance all aspects of your sport in order to achieve total enjoyment.
- Grooming is essential for the horse's physical well-being, and also for building a trusting relationship between horse and rider.
- The warm-up not only supples the muscles of horse and rider; it also provides them with the opportunity to re-establish their partnership.
- Rides in the countryside provide a time for both mental and physical stretching.
- Competitions are an opportunity to evaluate your progress.
  Your support system plays a central role in the balanced approach
- to competition.

FURTHER READING

Lynch, J., *Living beyond limits: Tao of self-empowerment*, (Walpole, New Hampshire, Stillpoint 1988).

Chapter 8 The Balanced Perspective

Millman, D. ' The arena of daily life', *No ordinary moments: Peaceful warrior's guide to daily life*, (Tiburon, California, H. J. Kramer 1992), pp.14-21.

Orlick, T. 'Overload and adaptation for life', In pursuit of excellence, (Champaign, Illinois, Human Kinetics 1990), pp.163-6.

CHAPTER 9
TOWARDS THE
LEAP OF FAITH

Far away there in the sunshine
are my highest aspirations. I may
not reach them, but I can look up
and see their beauty, believe in them,
and try to follow where they lead.
Louisa May Alcott

Throughout the course of this book, we have offered many suggestions on how to improve your riding, both in terms of performance and enjoyment. After explaining terminology in Chapter 1, we elaborated on the applications and benefits of imagery in Chapter 2. The philosophy behind imagery is simple: it is easier to achieve a dream if we can see it in our mind's eye. In our childhood, we may have been discouraged from activities such as day-dreaming, but there comes a time to polish up this rusty skill, and employ it in a positive and constructive way. This, in essence, is the skill that we have referred to throughout the book as imaging.

Turning the image in your mind into attainment requires much commitment on your part. However, once you have established a clear, challenging, yet realistic vision of where you want to go, you are in a position to pursue this vision via a series of challenging but attainable goals. Planning the route from goal to goal requires assistance from your trainer and support team. With their help you can produce a written statement defining your long-, medium- and short-term goals. Once the pursuit of these is in progress, the major objective is to stay the course.

If your imagination and the goals you set are the building blocks for your riding career, then you need to attain certain skills which will enable you to cement these blocks firmly in place. Chapter 4 took you one step closer to your objectives by explaining the necessary focusing and re-focusing skills. Here, we discussed how to refine your methods of concentration by learning how to cope with distractions. These were pro-actively planned for by deliberately incorporating them into your daily and weekly training. A further tool in this specific toolbox was the use of positive self-talk. Everyone experiences an internal monologue: this can be a voice that says 'well done', or it can be a critical, irritating sound that detracts from your performance. As you gain an awareness of occurrence, you can learn to edit it to your best advantage.

Learning to focus in a productive way, you become adept at utilizing activation and/or relaxation exercises as required. In Chapter 5, we explained how to relax your body, relax your mind, and then awaken your mind. To relax your body, the use of progressive muscle relaxation, eye exercises, and deep abdominal breathing was suggested. To relax the mind, the use of guided meditation – through imagery, suitable music, quiet surroundings, and dim lighting – was proposed. Tactics such as these are useful prior to a stressful training or competition experience. There are also times when you might feel sleepy, and have difficulty finding the mental energy to deal with challenges. During such times, we proposed the use of activation exercises such as trigger words, active guided imageries, energetic music, and physical stimulation.

Whilst in the process of learning such skills, you might experience moments of awkwardness and unease. With repetition, however, the exercises become simpler to follow. Once these skills have become part of your personal repertoire, you can adapt them to suit your personal style. You have then completed the learning cycle examined in Chapter 6.

Having worked through the difficult processes of learning so many new skills, you have all the components of the competitor's package discussed in Chapter 7. You can now see a pattern emerging, whereby each skill has a specific time, place, and application. At the highest levels of both physical and mental training, the athlete and the skill become one. However, during your pursuit of the highest level of skill you may, at some point, lose perspective of just why you are riding. Chapter 8 therefore offered a riding philosophy, and gave some suggestions of how to re-establish and maintain your love of horses and riding. It is when you have a balanced perspective to combine with your physical and mental skills that you are able to take the leap of faith and meet new challenges undaunted.

THE LEAP OF FAITH

The leap of faith is the action required to bridge the gap between being presented with a new challenge and meeting (overcoming) it. Each time you are confronted with a test, your initial reaction might be: 'Can I do it?' Every situation can be viewed either as a barrier, or as an obstacle to be leapt. On this basis, you can choose to progress, or to maintain the status quo. Choosing to move on, you begin to explore the available options. At this point, it is greatly encouraging to find support for your chosen course of action. In essence, it is easier to believe in yourself when others believe in you. Feeling confident, you are then free to shed all self-doubt and take the leap of faith.

Feeling confident, you are then free to shed all self-doubt and take the leap of faith.

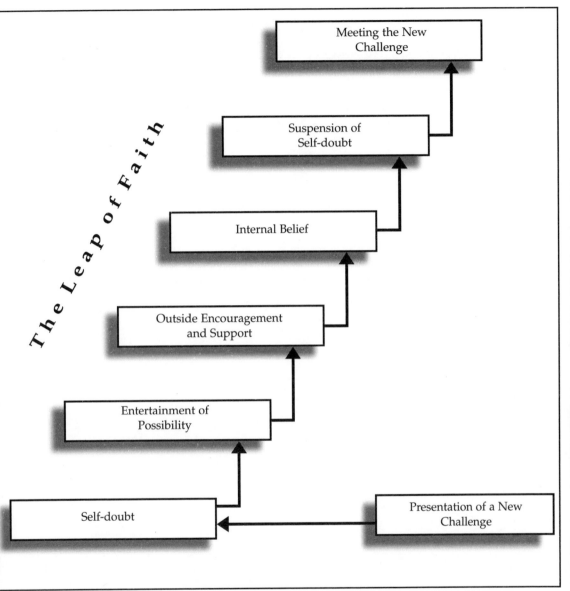

Figure 7: Steps to the Leap of Faith

A person can have the world's best trainer, the most talented and athletic horse, an abundance of technical and psychological skills, and yet still fall short of their goals. What is it that holds such a person back? Some answers might include a fear of success, a fear of failure, or a fear of risk-taking. These are natural feelings, found in most sports enthusiasts – including riders. Those who have achieved their goals have found a way to transcend such personal feelings and take the leap of faith. In doing so, these people free themselves from their limitations and become one with their sport. In conclusion, therefore, we maintain that it is your thoughts and beliefs which can either hold you back or set you free. We trust that you will make the choice that is best for you.